Memoirs of Margaret Baxter: Daughter of Francis Charlton and Wife of Richard Baxter : With Some Account of Her Mother, Mrs. Hanmer, Including a True Delineation of Her Character

Richard Baxter

MI

MRS. MARGA... BAX ER,

DAUGHTER OF FRANCIS CHARLTON, ESQ.

AND

WIFE OF MR. RICHARD BAXTER.

WITH

SOME ACCOUNT OF HER MOTHER, MRS. HANMER:

INCLUDING

A TRUE DELINEATION OF HER CHARACTER.

BY THE

Rev. RICHARD BAXTER.

TO WHICH IS ADDED,

AN APPENDIX:

CONTAINING

THE AUTHOR'S

Comparison between his Younger and his Riper Years;

An Account of

His Sentiments about Controversial Writings; his Temptations
and Difficulties; Improvements, Defects, and
Confession of his Faults.

"The memory of the just is blessed." Prov. x. 7.

LONDON :

RICHARD EDWARDS, CRANE COURT, FLEET STREET.

1826.

ADVERTISEMENT.

—◆—

THE following interesting piece of Female Biography was first published by the justly celebrated Reverend Mr. Baxter, in the year 1681, under the title of "A Breviat of the Life of Margaret, the Daughter of Francis Charlton, of Appley in Shropshire, Esq. and Wife of Richard Baxter." Having become exceeding scarce, it is again presented to the world, with the hope that it may be useful to many in the present day.

This Memoir exhibits in Mrs. Baxter a character so justly worthy of imitation for solid piety, active benevolence, and every social and domestic virtue, as at once to command love and respect. She was so eminently blessed with a spirit of philanthropy, an ardent and generous mind, a sound judgment, and refined sensibility, added to a highly cultivated intellect, that her company was eagerly sought, and greatly valued. With what ardour of mind she strove to alleviate the miseries and to increase the happiness of the poor, the afflicted, and the destitute, a perusal of the narrative will abundantly shew.

The account of the very excellent Mother of Mrs. Baxter, added to this edition, is taken chiefly from a Funeral Sermon, preached by Mr. Baxter at her decease, and published soon after, at his wife's particular request.

The APPENDIX, it is presumed, will be considered a pleasing addition to the memoir, containing an account of Mr. Baxter himself, written when advanced in years: The comparison he draws between his views when young and at mature age, is interesting, and worthy of the greatest attention.

The Notes have also been added, and may either be read with the narrative, or omitted, at the option of the reader: they are partly illustrative of some incidents not so fully understood without them; but they principally consist of Biographical Notices of several of Mr. Baxter's intimate friends mentioned in the memoir, and were mostly written by himself at different periods. They have been collected from his " Life and Times" in folio, from other parts of his writings, and other sources.

THE EDITOR.

LONDON, January 2, 1826.

THE

AUTHOR TO THE READER.

GOD having called away to his blessed rest
and glory, the spirit of the most dear companion of these last nineteen years of my life, or
near; I found in her last will a request, that I
should reprint five hundred of her Mother's
Funeral Sermon, written by me in 1661, being
now out of press, called, 'The Last Work of a
Believer, his Passing Prayer, &c.' Not only
her very great love and honour of her remembered Mother moved her to it, but the apprehension of the usefulness of that subject to
dying Christians; a subject about which her
soul was awakened the more, by the death of
many friends and excellent Christians taken
away this year. And the day somewhat excited her; for it was written by her on December 30, the same day which she kept secretly
as an anniversary remembrance of the sentence
of death from which she had been delivered;
and the same day when our dear friend Mr.
Corbet* lay dying. And I find some expectations of her own speedy death had some hand
in it.

* For an account of this good man, see page 57, *note.*

a 2

Being thus obliged by her request, mine own affections urged me to premise this breviat of her own life: written, I confess, under the power of melting grief, and therefore perhaps with the less prudent judgment; but not with the less, but the more truth: for passionate weakness poureth out all, which greater prudence may conceal. Conscionable men's histories are true; but if they be also wise, they tell us but some part of truth, concealing that which would do harm, and which the depraved world cannot bear without abusing it. But we that are less wise tell all the truth, too little regarding how men will receive it. And hence comes all history, which hath not evidence equal to natural, to be of less credit than most men think; while bad men lie, and good men leave out so much of the truth, as makes the rest to be as another thing than altogether it would appear.

And having purposed to write this breviat concerning my dear wife, God having the same year taken away two more of my ancient family, I wrote a breviat of their lives also: One was my excellent, holy mother-in-law, Mary, the daughter of Sir Thomas Hunks, widow to my dear Father. She was one of the most humble, mortified, holy persons that ever I knew; and lived in longing to be with Christ, till she was a hundred years old, want-

ing three or four, in full understanding, and at
last rejoicing in the triumphant frequent hearing and repeating the 91st Psalm.

The other was my old friend and house-
keeper, Jane Matthews, who lived in pious,
humble virginity, with eminent worth, to about
seventy-six or seventy-seven years, and died of
mere decay, without considerable pain or sickness, about a month or six weeks before my
wife.

To these I added a fourth, a breviat of the
life and death of that worthy mother of my
wife, as to the time since I knew her. But I
have cast by all these latter three, and much of
the first, by the counsel of wise friends, as
things which they think that strangers will not
make so great a matter of, as love and nearness
made me do. And I must confess, that God's
image is the same thing on all his children;
and when you have described one, you have
described all, as to the essentials. But (as in
faces and bodily strength) they so much differ
in integrals, degrees and accidents, that the
lives of some are far more exemplary and honourable to Christ their Lord, and their Christian profession than others are. And some are
so much blemished by errors, soul-diseases, and
miscarriages of life, yea, and injuries to the
Church of Christ, by their carnal animosities
and divisions, as rendereth the examples of the

more wise, holy, loving, peaceable, and patient Christians, the more conspicuous and
honourable by the difference.

On this account, finding young people naturally much delighted in history, and that for
want of better, abundance are quickly corrupted and ensnared by tale-books, romances, play-
books, and false or hurtful history, I have long
thought that true and useful history is of great
use to prevent such evils, and to many profitable ends : and that to young people it is very
profitable to begin with the Scripture history,
and next the lives of holy persons, and next to
read the true church historians, and the history
of our native country; Melchior Adamus in
Germany, Beza in his Icones, Thuanus and
many others in France, have done the church
this way great service, by a due commemora-
tion of exemplary persons. And such as Junius, Scultetus, Thuanus and others, who have
recorded the chief passages of their own lives,
have done a profitable work, though Mome's
will say, 'They publish their own praise in
pride.' There is no saying or doing any good
in the world, which bad men will not reproach,
or put an evil face on, or make an ill use of to
themselves. But he that reads such lives as
Bucholtzer's, Melancthon's, and their like, and
then readeth their church histories, will the
better discern that they were no liars.

As it is Satan's work to counterwork Christ

by the abuse and perversion of his own ordinances and means, (as to disgrace revelation by feigned revelation, and spirituality by false pretendings to the Spirit, and magistracy by wicked magistrates, and the ministry by worldly and ungodly ministers, and Christianity by hypocrite, false Christians); so he doth enervate the credit and use of history by false history. And how great use he hath made of this to promote Popery, he that readeth Jacobus de Voragine, and many other of their legends, or saints' lives and miracles, and such as Tympius and many more, besides their voluminous, deceitful histories of church, popes, and councils, may quickly find.

As to these little private histories of mine own family forementioned, I was loath to cast by my own mother-in-law's life, she being a person of so long and extraordinary holiness, living (long with Sir Robert Harley, whose lady was her cousin-german, and after at Shrewsbury, and after with my father and me, &c.) in so great communion with God, contempt of the world, and all its pomp and vanity, so great victory over the flesh, and so long desires to die, and especially in much constant, fervent, successful prayer that had marvellous answers, as very few Christians attain.

And I was loath to have cast by the narrative of my wife's mother, for some reasons not now to be mentioned, and because her daughter's extraordinary love to her made her just honour very dear to her: But her character is in the Sermon truly given you.*

But I am convinced by the judgment of my friends, that public things are most fit for public notice. And I feel that love, grief and nearness affect me with the matters that are so near me; and as it doth not much concern the world to know whether I am sick or well, dead or alive, or whether ever I had a being, (though it concerns me): so I should think of the concerns of my friends. Affection makes us think our own or our friends' affairs to be such, as the world should be affected with: I perceive this weakness and submit.

That which is left out of the narrative of my wife's life, is the occasions and inducements of our marriage, and some passages between some relatives and her, which the world is not concerned (yet at least) to know.

If this that is written seem useless to any, it will not hurt them if they leave it to others that find it more suitable to them. All things be not agreeable to all. That may be useful to persons of her own quality, which is not so to many others. To her nephews, and nieces, and some other kindred who were also near to her, and for whose sake above most others I write it, you cannot think that it will be altogether

---

* See an extract from this Sermon, pp. 113—134.

useless. O that they would all imitate her in all that is praiseworthy, and needful to themselves. The grand objection I foresee will be, that I seem but to predicate some of mine own good works by praising hers. And must I needs bury the memory of them as hers, for fear of the sting of such objectors? I have told them truly, it is not my own acts, but those that are properly hers that I there mention. It is not her giving of my money which I there recite, but that which either was her own and none of mine, or else procured by her for those uses; and the works such, in which I was but the executor of her will.

She is gone after many of my choicest friends, who within this one year are gone to Christ, and I am following even at the door. Had I been to enjoy them only here, it would have been but a short comfort, mixed with the many troubles which all our failings and sins, and some degree of unsuitableness between the nearest and dearest cause. But I am going after them to that blessed society, where life, light and love, and therefore harmony, concord and joy, are perfect and everlasting.

Reader, While I give thee but the truth, forgive the effects of age, weakness and grief. And if before I get over this (owned) passion, I publish also a few Poetical Fragments partly suited to the condition of some sick or sad afflicted friends, and partly to my own; if thou accept them not, forgive them only and neglect them. As the man is, such will be his thoughts and works. The Lord prosper our preparation for our great approaching change. To leave this world for ever, and enter upon an endless life, where we shall speed according to the preparations of this little inch of time, doth certainly bespeak the most serious thoughts, the wisest and speediest care and diligence, the most patient suffering, the most unwearied labour, the most frugal use of our time, the most resolute resistance to all temptations; and to the faithful the most joyful hopes.

RICH. BAXTER.

July 23, 1681.

MEMOIRS

OF

Mrs. MARGARET BAXTER.

CHAP. I.

Her Parentage, and the occasion of our Acquaintance.

1. Though due affection makes me willing to give the world a narrative which else I had omitted, yet the fear of God hath not so forsaken me, that I should willingly deliver any falsehood through partiality or passion : but as I knew more of this person than any other, for the good of the readers, and the honour of God's grace in her, I shall by God's assistance truly report the things which I knew.

2. We were born in the same county, within three miles and a half of each other ;* but she of one of the chief families in the county, and I but of a mean freeholder, called a gentleman for his ancestors' sake, but of a small estate, though sufficient : Her father, *Francis Charlton*, Esq. was one of the best justices of the peace in that county ; a grave and sober worthy man, but did not marry till he was aged and grey, and so died while his children were very young : who were three, of which the eldest daughter and the only son are yet alive. He had one surviving brother, who after the father's death, maintained a

---

* Mr. Baxter was born at *Rowton*, near High-Ercall, Salop, 12th Nov. 1615.

B

long and costly suit about the guardianship of the heir; this uncle, *Robert*, was a comely, sober gentleman; but the wise and good mother *Mary*, durst not trust her only son in the hands of one that was his next heir; and she thought that nature gave her a greater interest in him than an uncle had. But it being in the heat of the late civil war, *Robert* being for the Parliament, had the advantage of strength, which put her to seek relief at Oxford from the king, and afterwards to marry one *Mr. Hanmer*, who was for the king, to make her interest that way. Her house being a sort of small castle, was now garrisoned for the king. But at last, *Robert* procured it to be besieged by the parliament's soldiers, and stormed and taken; where the mother and the children were, and saw part of their buildings burnt, and some lie dead before their eyes; and so *Robert* got possession of the children.

But at last, she by great wisdom and diligence surprised them, secretly conveyed them to *Mr. Bernard's* in Essex, and secured them against all his endeavours.

3. The wars being ended, and she as guardian possessing her son's estate, took him (an only son) to herself, and used his estate as carefully as for herself; but out of it conscionably paid debts of her husband's, repaired some of the ruined houses, and managed things faithfully, according to her best discretion, until her son marrying, took his estate into his own hands.

4. She, being before unknown to me, came to Kidderminster (twenty miles), desiring me to take a house for her alone: I told her that I would not be guilty of doing any thing which should separate such a mother from an only son, who in his youth had so much need of her counsel, conduct, and comfort;

and that if passion in her, or any fault in him, had
caused a difference, the love which brought her
through so much trouble for him, should teach her
patience. She went home, but shortly came again,
and took a house without my knowledge.

5. When she had been there alone awhile, her unmarried daughter *Margaret*, (about seventeen or
eighteen years of age,) came after her from her brother's, resolving not to forsake the mother who deserved her dearest love; and sometime went to Oxford to her eldest sister, wife to *Mr. Ambrose Upton*,*
then canon of Christ Church. In this time the good
old mother lived as a blessing among the honest poor
weavers of Kidderminster, strangers to her, whose
company for their piety she chose before all the vanities of the world. In which time my acquaintance
with her made me know, that notwithstanding she
had formerly been somewhat passionate, she was a
woman of manly patience in her great trials; of prudence, piety, justice, impartiality, and other virtues.
Of her death anon. It is her daughter's case that
this is the prologue to.

* Wood, in his Athen. Oxon. observes of this gentleman, that
' he was one of those many that were this and the next year made
Fellows of Allsouls' College by the Visitors. In 1651, he became
by the favour of Oliver Cromwell, Canon of Christ Church, in the
place of Dr. John Mills, ejected for refusing the *Engagement*; but
being discharged of that place, about the 13th of March, 1659, to
make way for the said Mills, then restored by the Rump Parliament and secluded members added to them, he retired to London,
and lived sometime there a Nonconformist. Afterwards he went
into Ireland, got a place there belonging to the Customs, and lived
in good fashion for several years. Afterwards returning into England, he concluded his last days in London, and was buried at
Christ Church, in the City. He was one of the ancient family of
the Uptons in Devonshire.'

CHAP. II.

Of her Conversion, Sickness, and Recovery.

1. In her vain youth, pride, and romances, and company suitable thereto, did take her up ; and an imprudent, rigid governess that her mother had set over her in her absence, had done her hurt, by possessing her with ill thoughts of strictness in religion ; yet she had a great reverence for some good ministers, especially *Mr. Thomas Wright;** and she thought that she was not what she should be, but something better (she knew not what) must be attained.

In this case, coming to Kidderminster for mere love to her mother, she had great aversion to the poverty and strictness of the people there, glittering herself in costly apparel, and delighting in her romances. But in a little time she heard and understood what those better things were which she had thought must be attained.

And a sermon of *Mr. H. Hickman's*† at Oxford much moved her, on Isa. xxvii. 11 ; *It is a people of no understanding, therefore he that made them will not save them,* &c. The doctrine of conver-

---

* He was a man of extraordinary learning, ability, moderation, and peaceableness.

† Henry Hickman, B. D. Fellow of Magdalen College, and a celebrated preacher in Oxford : a smart disputant, and a man of excellent general learning. After he was ejected, he lived for some time privately in Worcestershire, preaching only occasionally ; and was afterwards minister of the English congregation at Leyden, in Holland, where he was generally much esteemed and respected. He lived to a good old age, and died there about the time of the Revolution. He was the author of several learned tracts.

sion, as I preached it as now in my "*Treatise of Conversion*," was received on her heart as the seal on the wax. Whereupon she presently fell to self-judging, and to frequent prayer, and reading, and serious thoughts of her present state, and her salvation.

2. A religious maid that waited on her, taking notice of this (for she kept all her matters so secret to herself, as was her great hurt all her life), acquainted her mother with it; and when it could be hid no longer, but her frequent closet-prayers were sometimes overheard, and her changed course of life discerned, her mother (who as far as I could discern, before loved her least of her three children,) began to esteem her as her darling.

3. I will here give you one of her self-judging papers, which I find since her death, upon her then sad convictions. When I had on Rom. viii. 9, told them how it may be known whether we have Christ's Spirit or not, she thus repeated the signs with her self-condemnation:

Mark 1. *The Spirit of Christ is the author of the Scriptures, and therefore suiteth your disposition to it, and guideth you by it.*

Judgm. 1. "I fear then I have not the Spirit of Christ; for I yet feel no love to God's word, nor closure with it as suitable to me; but I am questioning the truth of it, or at best quarrelling with it."

Mark 2. *The Spirit of Christ is from heaven, from God our Father, and leadeth us upward unto him. Its work is spiritual, of heavenly tendency, making us cry, 'Abba, Father,' and working the heart by uniting love to God.*

Judgm. 2. "It is not so with me, for I have a spirit tending only to selfishness and sin."

Mark 3. The Spirit of Christ uniteth us to Christ, and one another by love, and is against hatred, division, and abusing others.

Judgm. 3. "Mine then is the spirit of Cain, for I cannot endure any that are not of my opinion and way; and it inclineth me to malice, and unpeaceableness, and division."

Mark 4. The Spirit of Christ is a spirit of holiness, and doth not favour licentiousness in doctrine, or in life.

Judgm. 4. "Though I am for strict principles, I am loose in practice."

Mark 5. Christ's Spirit inclineth to love, humility, and meekness, and makes men stoop to each other for their good.

Judgm. 5. "None more uncharitable, proud and censorious than I."

Mark 6. The Spirit of Christ makes men little, low, and vile in their own eyes; it is pride that puffeth up.

Judgm. 6. "My self-conceitedness shews that I am unhumbled."

Mark 7. The Spirit of Christ doth work to the mortifying of the flesh, even all its inordinate desires, and to self-denial.

Judgm. 7. "I am a stranger to the work of mortification and self-denial. I can deny myself nothing but the comfort of well-doing. I cannot deny my sloth so far as to go to prayer when I am convinced of my necessity."

Mark 8. The Spirit of Christ is a prevailing Spirit, and doth not only wish and strive, but overcome the flesh as to its rule.

Judgm. 8. "The flesh prevaileth with me against the Spirit."

Mark 9. Christ's Spirit is the author of his worship

and ordinances, and suits the souls of believers to them, the *Word, Sacraments,* &c.

Judgm. 9. "They seem not suitable to my soul; I am against them, and had rather not use them, if I durst."

Mark 10. *Christ's Spirit is in all the saints, and inclineth them to holy communion with each other in love, especially to those in whom this Spirit most eminently worketh.*

Judgm. 10. "It is not thus with me: I desire not the communion of saints : my affections are most to those who are best to me, whether they have more or less of the Spirit.

"To go no further, it is now evident that I am a graceless person. Though all these things be imperfect in the best, and some are more wanting in one particular than in another; yet where all their contraries are predominant, as in me, that person is told by this sermon, that they are none of Christ's; how much doth my behaviour at this time make this appear, when I can with a hard heart, and a dry eye, and a steady hand, declare myself at present heir of everlasting woe! But the longest day will quickly come, though I strive to put it far from me."

4. It would be too long to recite a paper which I find next to this, containing the great necessity of self-judging, the reasons for it, the rules for performing it, and the due manner; especially in dangers, and before the Sacraments, or any conclusions of our state of grace.

5. But these convictions did neither die, nor pass unto despair, but to serious conversion ; yet put her to struggle hard against backwardness to secret du-

ties, and the forsaking of some vanities; but presently God seemed sharply to entertain this returning soul.   And while we were all rejoicing in her change, she fell into a cough, and seeming consumption, in which we almost despaired of her life.   The doctors judged it a consumption, arising from the obstructions of the vessels in the lungs, and corrupting the tender adjoining parts, and prescribed her the same medicines.   But all these, and change of air, did no good. I and my praying neighbours were so sorry that such a changed person should presently be taken away before she had time to manifest her sincerity, and do God any service in the world, that in grief they resolved to fast and pray for her; for former experience had lately much raised their belief of the success of prayer.   They had lately prayed for one that seemed demoniac, that after some years' misery, was suddenly freed of that disease.   They had oft prayed for me in dangerous illness, and I had speedy help. A young man falling into a violent epilepsy, and after all means remaining uncured, they set to fasting and prayer, and the second day he was suddenly cured, and never had a fit since.   God did not deny their prayers, though they were without book, and such as some deride as extemporate.   I was not with them in any of these, but laymen that were humble, praying persons.

But I was with them at prayer for this woman; and compassion made us all extraordinarily fervent, and God heard us, and speedily delivered her as it were by nothing, or by an altogether undesigned means.   She drank of her own inclination, not being directed, a large quantity of syrup of violets, and the next morning her pulse suddenly amended, her cough abated, and her strength returned in a short time.

CHAP. III.

The workings of her Soul in and after this Sickness.

1. SHE being of too timorous and tender a nature, and the sharp work of her repentance being yet upon her spirit; for death to come and seem to summon her away to eternity at such a season and unsettled state, must needs greatly increase her fears, when the strongest, long experienced Christians find it no easy work to die in peace and willing resignation. But she had still a concealing temper, which made it never the easier within.

2. When God had recovered her, her mother invited those that fasted and prayed for her, to keep a day of thanksgiving for her deliverance. I asked her what she would have us give thanks for particularly? and in the morning as we began, she (that was recovered) gave us in this following paper:

"My life hath been a life of very great mercies, and these have aggravated my sin in overlooking them. Some of those which God hath most affected my heart with, I shall here mention; but alas! with a heart very insensible of the greatness of them.

"1. My mother's restoration first I did thank God for; and next, for many mercies of mine own. Four times before this, I have been delivered from great danger of death.

"And now I desire to acknowledge his mercy in delivering me from this death-threatening disease, and that in answer to prayer I am here now in competent health to speak of the goodness of the Lord.

"2. I desire to acknowledge it a mercy that God

afflicted me; and though I cannot with the Psalmist say, *But now I keep thy statutes*, I can say, *Before I was afflicted I went astray*. And how many great sins God hath prevented by this affliction, I cannot tell; but am sure that God hath dealt very graciously with me; and I have had many comforts with my sufferings, which God hath not given to many of his beloved ones.

" 3. I desire to acknowledge God's great mercy to me in bringing me to this town, under so useful means of grace; and that at such a time when I was even ready to engage in a course of sin and vanity, beyond what I had formerly lived in. This mercy is much *greatened* by the time; for had the Lord brought me hither in infancy, and removed me at riper years, the mercy would not have been so great. And if I had gone longer on in a course of hardening sins, it had been less than now it is.

" 4. I desire to acknowledge it a great mercy, that I want no outward thing, but am enabled to be helpful unto others, and have all the temporal mercies that I can well desire, for my encouragement in the ways of God.

" 5. I desire to acknowledge it a great mercy, that God hath given me an interest in the hearts and prayers of so many of his faithful servants in this place.

" 6. I desire to acknowledge it a great mercy, that God hath made me the child of godly parents, and a child of many prayers.

" 7. I desire to acknowledge it a great mercy, which I can never be thankful enough for, that God hath given me a heart in any measure willing to acknowledge his mercies, and be thankful for them; and that notwithstanding all that sin and Satan hath done to hinder it, he hath made me desirous this day to give up myself and all that I have to him ; taking him only for my God and chief felicity.

"And now the requests that I desire you to make to God on my behalf, are these :

"(1.) That he will give me a more thankful soul, that I may praise him all my days.

"(2.) And an humble heart, that I may be taught of God, who looketh on the proud afar off.

"(3.) And a tender conscience, that I may fear to offend him, and hate all sin.

"(4.) And strength so to resist temptation, that I be not led by Satan to dishonour God, or to provoke him.

"(5.) And a meek and quiet frame of spirit, that I may be contented to bear the afflictions that God shall lay me under without murmuring or repining."

3. This being that which she gave us in, I find under her hand this secret renewal that same day of her covenant with God, which I annex :

"This being a day set apart for returning thanks to God for his mercy, in delivering me from the gates of death, these people being they that have earnestly supplicated the throne of grace on my behalf, I here now renew my covenant with Almighty God, and resolve by his grace to endeavour to get and keep a fresh sense of his mercy on my soul, and a greater sense yet of my sin. I resolve to set myself against my sin with all my might, and not take its part, or extenuate it, or keep the devil's counsel, as I have done, to the wronging of God, and the wounding of my own soul. I resolve by God's assistance to set upon the practice of known duty, and not to study shifts and evasions to put off those which are either troublesome, chargeable, or likely to render me dishonourable and vile in the eyes of the carnal persons of the world. And this I do upon these considerations, and for these reasons :

" (1.) My life hath been a life of great mercy. God hath preserved it more than this once, and hath done exceeding great things for me, which engageth me more than many others, though all rational creatures are obliged to live to God their Maker.

" (2.) God hath not only given me life, but in some measure ability and opportunity to do him service; yea, and already some encouragement in the hopes of the success of some of my poor endeavours. (*I suppose on some of her servants.*)

" (3.) God hath more engaged me to himself, by taking me into his family, and planting me in his garden; and watering me with the dew from heaven. He hath set me in a fruitful soil : he hath given me the high privilege of a part in the hearts and prayers of his people; and I may say that I live to speak it, that God is a God hearing prayers, and hath heard and answered them. Though the tempter be busy to make me think diminutively of this mercy, yet I must not, but must acknowledge the greatness of it.

" (4.) As all these and more engagements are upon me, so I am already engaged by the baptismal covenant to God the Father, Son, and Holy Ghost, as my God and chief good, and only happiness, and as my Redeemer, Head and Husband, and as my Sanctifier and Comforter; and I have renewed it in the sacrament of the Lord's-supper; and how can I go back that have thus far engaged myself, and daily receive from God more obligations? Yea, God will expect more from me than from many others. Let me therefore see that I be in good earnest with God, and think not to put him off with hypocrisy; let me not deceive myself, for God will not be mocked; what I sow, I shall reap: If I belong to God, though I suffer whilst I am in the body, they will be but light afflictions, and but for a moment; but the everlasting kingdom will be mine inheritance; and when this life is ended, I shall reign with Christ; I shall be freed from sin and suffering, and for ever rejoice with saints and angels. But should I prove an hypocrite, I lose my labour, I lose my God, and damnation with devils and damned ones will be my reward for ever, and this the greater as my mercies have been abundant and great.

"Therefore I here desire this day to renew my covenant with God, and to beg the prayers of this people that God will not leave me to myself, but help me, by the sufficient grace of Christ, to keep the covenant which I have made. And I intend to keep this paper by me, to help to remember me and quicken me to duty, and hinder me from sin, and encourage me to go on cheerfully against temptations, looking still to Christ, who forsaketh not those that by faith and repentance come to him.

"To all this let me add these considerations of the vanity of the creature, and of all false hopes.

"It is contrary to the nature of the creature to be our peace; they are our discomforts and troubles, further than they help to lead us to the Creator. Let me not forget the time when I seemed near death: What comfort had I then in creatures? What ease from them? Was not all my hope in God? All creatures shewed me that side on which *vanity* was written, and they had nothing which could satisfy my soul; though I had as much mercy in means and friends as I could possibly desire, yet all this was nothing to me; the trouble of parting with them was much more than the comfort of enjoying them; and so it will be with me still : which should teach me to keep my heart loose from the creature, and not over-love any thing on this side heaven. Why should my heart be fixed where my home is not? Heaven is my home; God in Christ is all my happiness; and where my treasure is, there my heart should be. Come away, O my heart, from vanity; mount heavenward, and be not dead, or dull, if thou wouldst be free from trouble, and taste of real joy and pleasure. Hath not experience yet taught thee, that creature-comforts, though they may be roses, have their pricks? Canst not thou be content to look on them, and smell them at a distance, and covet no other use while thou art in the garden where they grow, and be content to leave them there behind thee? If thou must needs have them in thy bosom, thou must scratch thy fingers to get them; and when thou hast them, though the smell awhile delight thee, they will quickly wither, and are gone. Away then, O my carnal heart, retire to God, the only satisfying object. There mayest thou love without all danger of excess! Let thy love to God be fixed and transcendent. Amen."

4. Though these were the strivings of her heart towards God, her fears and troubles did not so pass away; settled peace of soul doth seldom come quickly to young converts, though their sincere resolutions

may be settled. I find among her papers yet more of that day's work, upon her after-examination and review. Bear with the length, if I transcribe it as I find it under her hand.

"Christ saith, *In the world you shall have trouble, in me you shall have peace.* Something of both now I find at this time. This night, after returning thanks to God for my recovery, I find my heart sad, and trouble upon my spirits; and well it may be so; for the sins of this day have been very great: my heart hath not answered the expressions of thanks which have been uttered by the mouths of those that spake them to God. No, no, my heart hath not stirred, and been drawn out towards my God! The thoughts of his love have not ravished my soul. Alas! I scarce felt any holy spark to warm my soul this day. This day, which was a day of the greatest mercy of any in all my life; the day in which I have had an opportunity to give thanks for all the mercies of my life, and thanks itself is a greater mercy than the rest: all other mercies are to prepare for this: this is the work of a glorified saint, even a saint in heaven before the blessed face of God: it is his everlasting business to sing the songs of thanksgiving and praise to the Most High. But my thoughts have not been filled with the sweet foretastes of this blessed work, which I might have had this day! O God, I beseech thee forgive my sin, and lay not my deadness to my charge, but overlook all my transgressions, and look on me in Jesus Christ my Saviour. I am thine, Lord, and not mine own: this day I have under my hand and seal, in the presence of witnesses, nay in thine own presence (who art witness sufficient, were there no eye to see me, or ear to hear me). Thou Lord, that knowest all things, knowest that I have devoted my all to thee : take it, and accept my sacrifice : help me to pay my vows !*

---

* In the preface to a little volume of Poetical Fragments, published by Mr. Baxter in 1689, and which it appears he wrote principally on account of his wife, before their marriage, he thus speaks : ‘God having taken away the dear companion of the last nineteen years of my life, as her sufferings and sorrows long ago gave being to some of these Poems (for reasons which the world is not concerned to know), so my grief for her removal, and the revived sense of former things, have prevailed with me to publish them.’ He farther observes in a note at the end of the following Poem : ‘This covenant my dear wife in her former sickness subscribed with a cheerful will.’ In it she solemnly dedicates herself and all she possesses to her Divine Lord and Master; and it appears by her subsequent life that she never lost sight of this act of solemn dedication to God. John xii. 26.

THE COVENANT AND CONFIDENCE OF FAITH.

‘My whole, though broken heart, O Lord !
   From henceforth shall be thine !
And here I do my vow record :
   This hand, these words are mine.
All that I have, without reserve,
   I offer here to thee :
Thy will and honour all shall serve,
   That thou bestow’dst on me.
All that exceptions save I lose :
   All that I lose I save :
The treasure of thy love I choose ;
   And Thou art all I crave.
My God, thou hast my heart and hand :
   I all to thee resign.
I’ll ever to this covenant stand,
   Though flesh hereat repine.
I know that thou wast willing first ;
   And then mad’st me consent :
Having thus lov’d me at the worst,
   Thou wilt not now repent.

Wilt thou not accept me because I do it not more sincerely and believingly? O Lord, I unfeignedly desire to do it aright! O! wilt thou strengthen my weak desires! I believe, Lord help my unbelief.

Now I have quit all *self-pretence*,
  Take charge of what's thine own,
My life, my health, and my defence,
  Now lie on thee alone.
Now it belongs not to my care,
  Whether I die or live:
To love and serve thee is my share:
  And this thy grace must give.
If life be long, I will be glad,
  That I may long obey:
If short, yet why should I be sad,
  That shall have the same pay.
If Death shall bruise this springing seed,
  Before it come to fruit;
The will with thee goes for the deed;
  Thy life was in the root.
Long life is a long grief and toil,
  And multiplieth faults:
In long wars he may have the foil,
  That scapes in short assaults.
Would I long bear my heavy load?
  And keep my sorrows long?
Would I long sin against my God?
  And his dear mercy wrong?
How much is sinful flesh my foe,
  That doth my soul pervert;
To linger here in sin and woe,
  And steals from God my heart?
Christ leads me through no darker rooms
  Than he went through before:
He that into God's kingdom comes,
  Must enter by this door.
Come Lord, when grace hath made me meet,
  Thy blessed face to see:

Thou that canst make me what I am not, O make me what thou wouldst have me be! In thee there is all fulness, and to thee I desire to come by Christ. Wilt thou now cast me off, because I do it not *unreservedly*? Lord, I confess the devil tempteth, and the flesh saith, *Spare something: what! let all go?* And I find in me a carnal, selfish principle, ready to close with the temptation. But thou canst prevent and conquer all, and speak death to these corruptions, and bid the tempter be gone. It is thy pleasure here to suffer thy dear children to be tempted; but suffer not temptations to prevail against thy Spirit and grace. If temptation be like a torrent of water, to smother, quench, or hide the flame, yet wilt thou never let all the sparks of thy grace be put out in the soul where once thou hast truly kindled it. But, Lord, suffer not such floods to fall on my soul, where the spark is so small already, that it is even scarce discernible! O quicken it, and blow it up to a holy flame: most gracious God! O do it here, who hast done it for many a soul! O what have I said! That I have a spark of grace! Why the least spark is worth ten thousand times more thanks than I can ever express! And I have been dead and unthankful, as is before confessed! And is that a sign of

For if thy work on earth be sweet,
   What will thy glory be?
Then I shall end my sad complaints,
   And weary, sinful days;
And join with the triumphant saints,
   That sing Jehovah's praise.
My knowledge of that life is small;
   The eye of faith is dim:
But it's enough that Christ knows all;
   And I shall be with him."

grace! Unthankful, dead, and dull I have been, and
still am; but yet it must needs be from God's gift in
me, that I have any desires after him; and that this
day I have desired to devote myself to him, and that
I can say I would be more holy, and more heavenly,
even as the Lord would have me be. Nay, I do
know the time when I had none of these desires, and
had no mind to God, and the ways of godliness; and
do I not know that there be many in this condition,
who have no desires after Christ and holiness? Here
then is matter of comfort given me from him that
doth accept the desires of his poor creatures, even the
Lord Christ, who will not quench the smoking flax,
nor break the bruised reed. I see then that I have
yet matter of rejoicing, and must labour to be so
humbled for my remaining sins, as may tend to my
future joy in believing; but not so as to be discou-
raged and frightened from God, who is longsuffer-
ing and abundant in mercy. Rouse up thyself then
to God, my soul; humbly, but believingly repent
that thou hast been so unthankful, and insensible of
the benefits this day received: Up, up, and lie not
down so heavily; God hath heard prayers for thee,
and given thee life and opportunity to serve him.
He hath given thee all the outward mercies thy heart
can desire. He hath given thee dear, godly, able
friends, such as can help thee in the way to heaven;
yea, he hath set them to beg spiritual mercies for
thee, who prevailed for temporal for thee, and oft for
many others; why then shouldst thou not watch
and pray, and wait in hope that he hath heard their
prayers this day for thy soul, as formerly for thy
body? They are things commanded of God to be
asked; and we have his promise, that seeking we

shall find. It may be this night many of God's dear children will yet pray for my soul; I doubt not some will; and shall I not be glad of such advantage? I heard this day that *I must not forbear thanks, because the mercies are yet imperfect* (else we should never give thanks on earth). Though therefore my grace be yet but a spark, and weak, my body weak, my heart sad; all these administer matter of *thanks* and *praise*, as well as of *supplication*. Let me therefore keep close to both, they being the life of my life while I live here; and having daily need of supply from God, let me daily be with him, and live as in his presence: let him be the chief in all my thoughts, my heart and life. And let me remember to be earnest for my poor relations, and dear friends, and the church and people of God in general. And let me strive to keep such a moderate sense of sorrow on my soul, as occasion requireth. I have now cause of sorrow for parting with my dear friends, my father, my pastor. He is by Providence called away, and going a long journey: what the Lord will do with him, I cannot foresee; it may be he is preparing some great mercy for us, and for his praise; I know not but such a day as this may be kept here on his account. The will of the Lord be done, for he is wise and good; we are his own, let him do with us what he pleaseth; all shall be for good to them that love God. I have cause to be humbled that I have been so unprofitable under mercies and means; it may grieve me now he is gone, that there is so little that came from him left upon my soul. O let this quicken and stir me up to be more diligent in the use of all remaining helps and means. And if ever I should enjoy this mercy again, O let me make it appear that this night I was sensible of my neglect of it.

"And now here is comfort, that I have to deal with a God of mercy that will hear a poor repenting sinner; a God that will in no wise cast out those that come to him, but loveth whom he loveth, to the end. This is the God whom I have chosen and taken for my portion; the same God is his God, his guide and comforter. The whole world is but a house where God's children dwell a little while, till he hath fitted them for the heavenly mansions; and if he send them out of one room into another to do his work, and try their obedience; and if he put some in the darkest corners of his house, to keep them humble, though he separate those that are most beloved of each other, it is but that they may not love so much as to be loath to part and come to him who should have all their love. However it fareth with his children in this house (or howling wilderness), the time will come, and is at hand, when all the children shall be separate from the rebels, and be called home to dwell with their Father, their Head and Husband; and the elect shall all be gathered into one. Then farewell sorrow, farewell hard heart! farewell tears and sad repentance! And then blessed saints that have believed and obeyed! never so unworthy, crowned thou must be! This was the project of redeeming love! When the Lord shall take our carcases from the grave, and make us shine as the sun in glory, then, then shall friends meet and never part, and remember their sad and weary nights and days no more! Then may we love freely! What now is wanting to dispel all sorrow from my

heart? Nothing but the greater hopes that I shall
be one of this number. This, this can do it. No
matter if I had no friend near me, and none on earth;
if God be not far from me, it is well enough; and
whatever here befals the church and people of God,
it is but as for one day, and presently the storm will
be all over. Let me therefore cast all my care on
God : Let me wait on him in the way of duty, and
trust him : Let me run with patience the race that
is set before me, looking to Jesus, the Author and
Finisher of my faith, and believingly go to him in all
my troubles; and let me so labour here, that I may
find rest to my soul in the rest that remaineth for the
people of God.

"Rest! O sweet word! The weary shall have
rest, they shall rest in the Lord.

"*April* 10, on *Thursday* night at twelve of the
clock; a day and night never to be forgotten by *the
least of all God's mercies, yea, less than the least,
Thy unworthy, unthankful, and hard-hearted creature,*

M. Charlton."

5. Is not here in all these papers (which I saw not
till she was dead) a great deal of work for one day,
besides all the public work of a thanksgiving-day?
If I should give you an account of all her following
twenty-one years, what a volume would it amount
to! If you ask why I recite all this, which is but
matter well known to ordinary Christians; I answer,
1. It is not as matter of *knowledge*, but of *soul-
workings* towards God. 2. Is not this extraordinary
in a convert of a year, or few months standing? 3.
The love of God, and her, makes me think it worth
the publishing : they that think otherwise may pass

it by ; but there are souls to whom it will be savoury and profitable.

6. Yet she continued under great fears, that she had not saving grace, because she had not that degree of holy affection which she desired : and before in her sickness, her fears increased her disease and danger. I will here for the use of others in the like case, recite some scraps of a letter of counsel, as I find them transcribed by herself.

"I advise you to set more effectually to the means of your necessary consolation ; your strange silent keeping your case to yourself, from your mother and all your friends, is an exceeding injury to your peace. Is it God or Satan that hindereth you from opening your sore, and make you think that concealment is your wisdom ? If it be pride that forbids it, how dare you obey such a commander ? Many of our sores are half healed when well opened : if prudence foresee some forbidding inconvenience, you have prudent friends, and two prudent persons may see more than one. But because you will not tell us, I will disjunctively tell it you.

"1. Your trouble of soul is either some *affliction*. 2. Or some *sin*. 3. Or the doubt of your *sincerity* and true grace.

"I. If it be *affliction*, dare you so indulge, impatience, as to conclude against your future comforts, while you have God's love and title to salvation ? Dare you say that these are of so small weight, that a cross like yours will weigh them down ? and that you will not rejoice in all the promises of life eternal, till your cross be removed ?

"II. If it be *sin*, it is either past or present: if

past, why do you not repent, and thankfully accept your pardon? If *present*, it is *inward corruption*, or outward transgression. Whichever it be, if you love it, why do you grieve for it, and groan under it? If you grieve for it, why are you not willing to leave it, and be holy? If you are willing to leave it, and would fain have God's grace in the use of his means, to make you holy, this is the true nature of repentance. And why then are you not thankful for grace received, for pardon, adoption, and your part in Christ, more than you are troubled for remaining sin? Should none rejoice that have sin to trouble them, and keep them in a daily watch and war? Read Rom. vii and viii. if you will see the contrary: *If any man sin, we have an advocate with the Father, Jesus Christ the righteous, and he is the propitiation for our sins.* Dare you refuse your comforts on such reasons as would deny comfort to all the world? He that saith he hath no sin is a liar. And will you for this deny the known duty of thanks and praise for all that you have received? You have been taught to difference between cause of doubting, and cause of *filial humiliation.* And if it were any particular sin that needs particular help and counsel, why do you not open it for help, which it is probable would do more against it, than many years' secret trouble and dejection alone would do.

"III. If it be *doubts of your sincerity and grace,* why do you refuse to reason the case, and say what it is that persuadeth you that you are graceless, that we may try it by the Word of God? What evidence is it that you want? You have confessed that sometimes you are convinced of sincerity; and can you so easily deny what you have found, as to conclude yourself so miserable as you do? Should all do thus that have not constant apprehensions of their evidence, and whose assurance is hindered by imperfections? You have heard the contrary.

"But suppose that you have yet no saving grace or part in Christ, why stand you complaining, whilst Christ stands entreating you to accept his mercy? Is he not in good earnest? The offer is free; it is not your purchase and merit, but *consent*, that will prove your title. Why do you *complain*, and not *consent* even to the baptismal covenant? Or if you *consent*, why do you complain as if Christ's promise were not true, or as if *consent* were not a proof of saving faith? If you confess that you should not doubt and be dejected on such terms, methinks the cure should be half wrought. Dare you indulge it while you know it to be your sin? Have you not sin enough already? And is it not unkindness to deny so great a mercy as the converting grace which you so lately felt, and to suspect his love who is love itself, and hath so largely expressed his love to you? Would you easily believe that your mother would kill you for such defects as you fear that God will damn you for? Yea, though she were perfectly just and holy? Is it congruous to hear ministers tell men from Christ, that he beseecheth them to be reconciled to God, and will refuse none that are willing of his grace and cure; and at the same time to hear such as you almost ready to despair, as if God would not be reconciled, nor give grace to them that fain would have it, but will be inclined to reject humbled souls?

"Reason not for your distrustful fears and sorrows, but still disown them and accuse them, and

C

then they will vanish by degrees and die : yea, then you will sure oppose them yourself, and God will help you. Can you look that God should help you against the sin which you plead for, and defend? If faith and love be the vital graces, distrust of God, and denying his love, must not be defended as no sin. As the ungodly cannot expect the grace which they refuse, so how can you expect the peace which you oppose, and say as Psal. lxxvii ; *My soul refuseth to be comforted*; and say of your passionate fear and grief, as *Jonas* of his anger, *I do well to be angry, even unto death.* Be convinced that Christ is yours, if you accept him and consent ; and then that comfort is your interest, right and duty ; and then you will do more to comfort yourself, than I am endeavouring when I chide you for your fears. Sure sinful sorrow is no desirable thing, nor to be pleaded for ; you durst do nothing to the murder of a friend, no, nor to his grief ; and you are bid to love your neighbour as yourself. Away then with your weakening griefs and troubles, *lest they prove a degree of self-murder.* If you care for yourself, the comfort of your mother and friends, and the honour of the unspeakable riches of God's grace, at least own it to be your duty to oppose sinful fear, and to rejoice in God, and serve him with delight and cheerful praises, and do your best against all that is against this duty. And suffer not your sore to fester by your silence ; but open your case to some one that is able to help you impartially to try it by the Word of God, and to pray with you that God will mercifully discover your infirmities, and the remedy. It were but wisdom to conceal your case from others, if you can well be cured without their help."

7. Some strivings against her fears and sorrows I find next in this paper following, dated by her, *April* 3.

"The sadder my present condition is, the greater is the mercy that I am yet alive : why then should I not give God thanks for that, and beg the rest which yet I want?   And though my life seem but a burden to me sometimes, it is my great mistake; for the greatest afflictions are nothing to hell-torments : were they as great as ever any had; while I am alive on this side eternity, there is hope. The time of grace is yet continued; if I be found in mercy's way, I know not but God may yet be gracious, and give in my soul as he hath done my life at his people's prayers; for I cannot but look on my life as an answer to their prayers. And sure they desired my life only that I might live to God. I desired it myself on no other terms. It was my earnest request that I might not live, if not to him. Why then should I be persuaded by Satan to think that God will not give me grace as well as life? May I not rather be encouraged with patience to wait for further mercy? It is a mercy that I am in any measure sensible of my danger, and have any desire to be holy. I will therefore stir up my soul to thankfulness, and be humbled that I can be no more thankful. I will acknowledge the mercy I have received, and the probability of future mercy: and this by God's assistance the devil shall not hinder me from doing."

8. I will add one of her papers, containing her resolutions after her recovery, in some few particulars.

" *December* 30, was my worst day; I did not then
think to be alive this day; I ought not to forget it.
On *January* 1, *New-Year's-day*, I first bled at the
nose largely, and after mended. The fourth day was
kept in humiliation for me. *April* 10, was a day of
thanksgiving.

" When I thought I should die, I was more than
ordinarily sensible of my unprofitable life; and had
such convictions as usually people in my condition
have; and I then made many resolutions as in such
cases others do. I remembered that I had heard
much of the promises that many made in sickness,
which they never performed; and I thought it was
gross hypocrisy to speak now of that which I was
past performing (as I thought); but that I were better write down my purposes, and discover them if
God recovered me, that they might be as strong an
engagement on me, as if I had spoken them to men.*

---

* The following Poem is another of those written by Mr. Baxter for the comfort and encouragement of his afflicted friend, and is
taken from the Poetical Fragments. It contains a lively description
of her state of mind at this period, and points out the progress of
her Christian experience, commencing with a penitent confession of
her sinful nature; her sincere repentance and earnest desire for
God's pardoning love and mercy through Christ Jesus; her prayer
to be enabled to keep her covenant (before alluded to); and at
last to triumph over death and the grave. It is here given at length.

THE PRAYER OF THE SICK, IN A CASE LIKE HEZEKIAH'S.

The First Part.

'ETERNAL GOD, whose name is Love:
   Whose mercy is my hope and stay;
O hear and help me from above,
   That in distress to thee do pray,

"I. I resolved that I would endeavour to get and keep a sense of that great mercy of God's restoring me from the peril of threatened death, in answer to prayer; which was the greater, in that God threat-

Ashamed to lift up my face,
    Hence from the dust to thee I cry:
Though I have sinn'd against thy grace,
    Yet unto it alone I fly.
I was at first in sin conceiv'd,
    Then liv'd a vain and sinful life:
Rebellious flesh which I receiv'd
    Is still against thy grace in strife.
Long it was, LORD, alas, too long,
    Before I knew myself or thee:
Vanity rul'd my heart and tongue:
    And O that yet my soul were free!
But while I sinned thou wast kind,
    And sent'st thy word and spirit of grace;
Thy light did change my darkened mind,
    And shewed me my wretched case.
Though I drew back, thou didst prevail:
    And I gave up myself to thee.
Thou undertook'st for wind and sail;
    Both ship and pilot thou wouldst be.
I turn'd my back on worldly toys;
    And set my face towards glory's shore;
Where thou hast promis'd highest joys,
    And blessedness for evermore.
I took my leave of sin and earth;
    What I had lov'd, 1 now did hate:
Ashamed of my former birth,
    I gave my life a newer date.
But since that time how I am tost?
    Afraid of every storm and wave:
Almost concluding I am lost,
    As if thou wouldst not help and save.

ened to take me hence when I was but in the birth,
and had scarce well begun to live. This mercy I
promised to be thankful for, and to acknowledge
other mercies as God should make me able.

If I look out beyond thine ark,
  Nothing but raging seas I see :
On this side heav'n all's deep and dark :
  But I look further unto thee.
Censures, and scorns, and frowns I bear :
  Storms which before I never found ;
And yet all these I should not fear,
  If all at home were safe and sound.
But thy displeasure wounds my heart :
  I have but two parts, flesh and soul :
Both of thy wrath do bear their part ;
  And thou hast left me neither whole.
              The Second Part.
All this is just, Lord, I confess ;
  I staid too long ere I came in :
And how should healing grace do less,
  When I brought with me so much sin ?
Much pride and vanity I kept :
  Too oft my heart was looking back :
Though God stood by me, yet I slept :
  Heav'n was at hand ; yet I grew slack.
Spare Lord, and pity thy poor dust !
  That fled into thy ark for peace !
O cause my soul on thee to trust !
  And do not my distress increase.
O keep up life and peace within !
  If I must feel thy chastening rod !
Yet kill not me, but kill my sin ;
  And let me know, thou art my God.
Folly dwelt in my childish breast ;
  Sin robb'd me of my youthful days ;
Let not thy wrath cut off the rest,
  And stifle thine intended praise.

"II. I resolved that I would endeavour to be in a
fixed state and way of duty; and, in order to this I
would take advice of one who is, I conceive, most
fit to advise me. And I resolve by God's assistance,

Whilst I forgot thee, thou didst bear :
  Thy kindness did invite me home :
O rack me not with grief and fear!
  Kill me not Lord, now I am come.
The silent dust speaks not thy fame,
  Nor in dark graves art thou renown'd :
The living saints declare thy name,
  And in thy church thy praises sound.
Yet let me with thy household dwell;
  Though I be number'd with thy poor :
And with thy saints thy wonders tell,
  Although I sit behind thy door.
Set not thy strength against frail man!
  O turn not yet this flesh to clay !
My life, thou know'st, is but a span,
  If I should see the longest day.
Break me not all to pieces, Lord ;
  Or else let each piece have a tongue,
To cry, till thou relief afford,
  But not to say, thou dost me wrong.
Pity this poor unworthy soul,
  That here devotes itself to thee :
Resolve my doubts ; my fears control ;
  And let me thy salvation see.
O let that love which gave me groans,
  And taught my needy soul to pray,
Remove my fears, and hear the moans
  Which sorrow breathes forth night and day.

The Third Part.

Why art thou, fainting soul, cast down,
  And thus disquieted with fears?
Art thou not passing to thy crown,
  Through storms of pain, and floods of tears!

that I will not consult with flesh and blood, nor study
my carnal interest, but resolvedly set on the way of
my duty, and freely discourse my thoughts, so far as
is requisite to my just advice. And that I will speak

Fear not, O thou of little faith!
　　Art thou not in thy Saviour's hand?
Remember what his promise saith :
　　Life and death are at his command.
To him I did myself intrust,
　　When first I did for heav'n embark :
And he hath proved kind and just :
　　Still I am with him in his ark.
Couldst thou expect to see no seas,
　　Or feel no tossing wind or wave?
It is enough that from all these
　　Thy faithful Pilot will thee save.
Lord, let me not my covenant break!
　　Once I did all to thee resign :
Only the words of comfort speak,
　　And tell my soul that *I am thine.*
It's no death when souls hence depart,
　　If thou depart not from the soul:
Fill with thy love my fainting heart,
　　And I'll not fading flesh condole.
Health is but sickness with thy frowns :
　　Life with thy wrath is worse than death :
My comforts thy displeasure drowns,
　　And into groans tunes all my breath.
Where is that faith, and hope, and love,
　　By which thou markest all thy saints?
Thy joys would all my grief remove,
　　And raise this heart that daily faints.
Am I the *Jonas?* dost thou mean
　　To cast me out into the deep?
It shall not drown, but make me clean :
　　Until thou raise me, there I'll sleep.

my reasons and heart-risings against any thing that is propounded to me, which I judge unmeet. And I resolved when I saw my duty, cheerfully to do it, and keep a sense of the sweetness and obligations of God's love and mercy.

"III. I resolved to pray and labour for a true sense of the sins of this nation in general; and in particular of the sins of my relations, and of my own. And that till it please God to give me cause of rejoicing on the behalf of my relations, and of my own soul's recovery and spiritual welfare, I will continue with humiliation to supplicate the Lord. And though I would not shut out a greater duty by a lesser, yet I will avoid all manner of feastings as much as I well can, and all noxious, sensual delights; and when I must be present, I will use some mortifying restraint. And this I would do in my habit, and all other things, but that I would lay no snare on myself, by renouncing what occasions may oblige me to; but by all means I would strive to keep upon

O death! where is thy poisonous sting!
  O grave! where is thy victory?
Thy dust shall shortly rise and sing
  God's praise above the starry sky.
My God, my love, my hope, my life!
  Shall I be loath to see thy face?
As if this world of sin and strife,
  Were for my soul a better place?
O give my soul some sweet foretaste
  Of that which I shall shortly see!
Let faith and love cry to the last,
  Come Lord, I trust myself with thee.
    John xi. 14, or 16.
O let not unbelieving Thomas' words
Be now my answer: but my dearest Lord's. Amen.'

my heart a sense of my friends' danger and my own.

"IV. I resolve, if Providence concur, to go to London as soon as I can after the day of thanksgiving, for the reasons mentioned in another place."

9. What these reasons were, I find not. This following fragment of hers, hints something of it.

"I begin already to be sensible of my misusing the helps which God had given me; I know now how I should love ordinances and means of grace, and to what end; not to break my heart when Providence removeth them from me, or me from them; but I should love them for God, and use them for him, and expect my greatest comfort from him, and not from men and means themselves: this is no more than what I thought I had known long ago, but I never knew it indeed till now. And now I do but begin to know it. When I felt my heart ready to sink under a burden of sorrow, God was pleased to ask me what I ailed. Was my condition worse than ever? Had I less hopes of his love than heretofore? If not, why do I mourn more than when I lay under that curse? What is it that I have chosen for my hope and happiness? Is that lost and gone? Am I left in such a place or case as God cannot be found in if I truly seek him; or that God cannot sweeten with his presence? If not, why do I not contentedly thank God for what I have already had? I cannot say it is better that I had never had it, than now to leave it: no, I must be willing to submit to God, and be humbled in the sense of my abuse of mercy, so far as it may quicken me to diligence for the time to come. And if ever God more trust me with such treasure as once I had, I will strive to shew that I better know the worth of it than I did before. My thoughts often tell me, that if I were but in a condition in which I had opportunity to serve God with more cost to the flesh than I here do, it would either shew my hypocrisy, or give me more assuring evidence that I am indeed sincere."

10. And it is a useful note that I find added to this by her.

"If my trouble be for my sin, (1.) My care will be more for the removing of my sin, than of the affliction.

"(2.) And if God should take away the affliction, it would not content me, unless sin be taken away, and my heart amended.

"(3.) If it be sin that I am troubled for, it will be my great care not to sin in my trouble.

"(4.) And if it be my sin that troubleth me, I have the more cause to submit to God's hand, and silently bear the punishment of my iniquity; it shameth murmuring, when we truly look on sin the cause, though it bring the wholesome sorrow of repentance.

"(5.) And if I mourn for fear lest God be departing, I should seek him, and cleave the closer to him, and not depart from God, and then he will not depart from me."

11. I will conclude this chapter with a country poem of her honest kinsman *Mr. Eleazer Careswell,* of *Sheffnall,* in *Shropshire,* whom I never knew to poetize but now that tender love and passion taught him; it signifieth these, though it want the flowery

part.   Her danger of death so near to her conversion,
was very grievous to him.

MARGARET CHARLTON.

ANAGRAM.

ARM TO LATER CHANGE.

THE prudent soul refin'd from earth, doth ever
Arm to her later change, and fears it never.
Those glittering monarchs who seem to command
This ball, shall be by death's impartial hand
Put out, and doom'd to an eternal state,
(No mortal sinner can decline this fate.)
Death conquers sceptre-swaying kings; but I
Shall conquer death, being now arm'd to die.
Arm soul for this one change, and wed thy heart
To Christ, and then no death shall ever part
Your joined souls; and thou, because that He
Hath life, of life shalt still possessed be.
Death will but this snarl'd knot of life untie,
To unite souls in a more blessed tie,
When faith, renewing grace, repenting tears,
Hath clear'd the soul from filth, and she appears
Unspotted, holy, pure, invested in
Christ's milk-white snowy robes, quite freed from sin.
Wholly deliver'd from this fleshly thrall,
And hell's black monarch, and adorn'd with all
God's perfect grace : triumphantly these sing,
Death and hell conquer'd are by Christ our King.
Faith, hope, and love, such souls now fortify,
And armed thus, why should we fear to die?
Tho' death divorce those long-acquainted friends,
And lodge earth in the earth ; the soul ascends
To those high, glorious regions, where she
With Christ and blessed souls shall ever be.
Soul-troubling sin shall then molest no more,
Which clogg'd, which wounded her so long before.

Poor souls go fetter'd here with flesh and sin,
Death doth her great deliverance begin.
Thy soul renew'd by grace, shall quickly see
How blest a change that day will bring to thee.
Death shall those weeping eyes dry up and close,
And pained weary flesh to rest repose.
The grave will be a safe and quiet bed,
To that frail body when the soul is fled.
This aching head shall there be laid to rest,
Whilst thy glad soul of glory is possessed.
As banish'd griefs end in that quiet sleep,
Thy dust is holy, it thy Lord will keep
Till the last trumpet sound; and he shall raise
The just and unjust at the last of days.
Then the refined body shall again
Its late dislodged soul re-entertain;
And re-united chant well-tuned lays
Unto the Lamb, whose soul-enamouring lays
Shall ravish saints with blessed, perfect joy,
Freed from whatever would their rest annoy.
Where they with flaming love and pleasure sing
Holy, melodious praise to God their King,
Rise then my soul; thy thoughts from earth estrange;
The first is wrought, *Arm to thy later change.*

Thus the good man's affections worked to prepare his dear kinswoman for death; but he died, and most of his, before her.

CHAP. IV.

Some Parcels of Counsel for her Deliverance from this distressed Case, which I find reserved by her for her Use.

1. WHILE in her languishing, and after it, she was still cast down, condemned herself as a graceless wretch, and her good mother and friends afraid that

her grief would increase her sickness, as it did their sadness; and yet she obstinately concealed it from all, save a few sad complaints to one person, who wrote thereof some fragments which she extracted for her use; I shall here recite them for others that have the same fears.

2. The miscarriage of a relation troubling her, this was set down.

"When God hath done so much for you, will you leave it in the power of an inconstant creature to trouble you, and rob you of your peace? Is the joy in the Holy Ghost so subject to the malice of your enemies, *or the weakness of your friends?* Delight yourself in an all-sufficient constant God, and he will be to you a sufficient, constant delight, and will give you the desires of your heart. I see you are yet imperfect in self-denial, while you are too sensible of unkindnesses and crosses from your friends, and bear them with too much passion and weakness: know you not yet what the creature is, and how little is to be expected from it? Do you not still reckon to meet with such infirmities in the best, as will be injurious to others, as they are troublesome to themselves? It is God that we most wrong, and yet he beareth with us; and so must we with one another. Had you expected that creatures should deal as creatures, and sinners as sinners, how little of this kind of trouble had you felt. Especially take heed of too much regard to matters of mere reputation, and the thoughts of men; else you are like a leaf in the wind that will have no rest. Look on man as nothing, and be content to approve yourself to God; and then so much honour as is good for you, will follow as the shadow. If every frailty and unkindness of the best friends must be your trouble, it is to be impatient with the unavoidable pravity of mankind; and you may as well grieve that they were born in sin, and made your acquaintance. And it should be used as a mercy to keep you from inordinate affections to friends. It is a mercy to be driven from creature-rest, though it be by enemies. Keep a fixed apprehension of the inconsiderableness of all these little things that cross you, and turn your eye to God, to Christ, to heaven, the things of unspeakable weight, and you will have no room for these childish troubles.

" Yet turn not the discovery of this your weakness, into dejection, but amendment; I perceive you are apter to hold to the sense of your own distempers, than to think what counsel is given you against them."

3. On another occasion she recorded these words.

"How hard is it to keep our hearts in going too far even in honest affections toward the creature, while we are so backward to love God, who should have all the heart, and soul, and might. Too strong love to any, though it be good in the kind, may be sinful and hurtful in the degree. 1. It will turn too many of your thoughts from God, and they will be too oft running after the beloved creature. 2. And by this exercise of thoughts and affections on the creature, it may divert and cool your love to God, which will not be kept up, unless our thoughts be kept more to him; yea, though it be for his sake that you love them. 3. It will increase your sufferings, by interesting you in all the dangers and troubles of those whom you overlove."

4. When she seemed to herself near death.

"You now see what the world and all its pleasures are, and how it would have used you, if you had had no better a portion, and God had not taught you a happier choice. Providence now tells you that they are vanity, and if overvalued, worse; but if you learn to see their nothingness, you will be above the trouble of losing them, as well as the snares of too delightful enjoying them. Pardon all injuries to men, and turn your thoughts from them, and keep your heart as near as possible to the heart of Christ, and live as in his arms, who is usually sweetest when the creature most faileth us, if we do but turn our hearts from it to him."

5. Another time.

"Can you find that you are resolvedly devoted to Christ, and yet doubt whether Christ be resolvedly and surely yours? Are you more willing or more faithful than he?"

Hence she gathered herself as followeth.

" When I read the evidence of my self-resignation to Christ, I should as it were see Christ standing over me with the tenderest care, and hear him say, ' *I accept thee as my own.*' For I must believe his acceptance, as I perform my resignation. O what is he providing for me! What entertainment with

him shall I shortly find!   Not such as he found with
man, when he came to seek us; it is not a manger,
a crown of thorns, a cross, that he is preparing for
me: when I have had my part of these in following
him, I shall have my place in the glorious Jerusalem."

6. This fragment she wrote next.

"For the sake of your own soul, and life, and
friends, and for the honour of that tender mercy and
free grace which you are bound to magnify, let
not Satan get advantage against your peace and
thankfulness to God, and the acknowledgment of his
obliging love.   Let him not on pretence of humiliation, turn your eyes on a weak, distempered heart,
from the unspeakable mercy which should fill your
heart with love and joy, notwithstanding all your la-
mented infirmities.   You perceive not that it is Satan
that would keep you still under mournful sadness,
under the pretence of repentance and godly sorrow.
You are not acquainted with his wiles.   You have
cause of sorrow, but much more of joy.   And your
rejoicing in God's love would please him better than
all your sad complaints and troubles, though he despise not a contrite spirit.   I charge it on your conscience, that when you are in prayer, you confess and
lament your distrustful, suspicious, unthankful, uncomfortable thoughts of God and Jesus Christ, more
than all your want of sorrow for him.   And you trouble yourself for such kind of sins, *the honesty of whose
occasion may give you more comfort than the fault
doth sorrow.*   I know we have not our comfort at
command.   But see that your endeavour and striving

be more for a comfortable than for a sorrowful frame of spirit.

"Two things I must blame you for, 1. That you take the imperfections of your duties and obedience, to be greater reasons for discomfort, than the performance and sincerity are reasons for comfort; as if you thought any thing were perfect here, or that it were better do nothing than do it imperfectly: or as if you would have no comfort till you can perform such duty and obedience as hath no need of pardon and a Saviour; and so no man living might have any comfort in any thing that he doth.

"2. That when unreasonable fears and troubles are upon you, and troubling thoughts are still upon your mind, you say that *you cannot help it nor turn, your thoughts away to any thing else.* I know you have not an absolute power over your thoughts, but some you have; why else hath God made a law for our thoughts, and laid so much duty on them, and forbidden their sin so much? Much may be done, if you will be resolute.

"Think whether Christ came from the Father to bring tidings of sadness and despair, or of great joy; and whether angels preached not *glory to God in the highest, on earth peace, and to men goodwill?* And whether *faith, hope,* and *love,* which are the things which Christ will work on souls, be not more powerful to destroy your sins, than despair or discouragement of mind?

"And because you complain so much of sin, I ask you, why doth not your conscience more accuse you of the sin of unthankful denying or extenuating the mercies of God, and no more magnifying them? And for overlooking so much the meritorious righ-

teousness of Christ, while you complain for want of
more of your own? I would not deceive you, by
telling you that you need none in yourself, and that
all your righteousness is out of you in Christ: I
know that your righteousness must exceed that of
the Pharisees, and the unrighteous shall not inherit
the kingdom of God, and that he that doth righteousness is righteous: but at what bar or tribunal?
Only at that of grace which *supposeth the reconciling,
pardoning righteousness of Christ :* it is not at the bar
of rigorous justice, according to the law, which requireth *innocence* to justification; there *Christ only* is
your *righteousness;* and you have none, and must
dream of none but that which floweth from his, and
stands in subordination to it, and is your title to it,
and improvement of it, *even your thankful accepting
a free-given Saviour, Head and Lord, and pardon and
the Spirit to sanctify you more, and fit you for communion with God and for glory ; esteem most, choose first,
and seek most the love of God the Father, the grace of
Christ, and the communion of the Holy Ghost,* and this
subordinate righteousness will certainly prove the
meritorious, perfect righteousness of Christ to be for
you, instead of a perfect righteousness of your own.
There is no defect in his sacrifice or merits; if you
wanted a title to Christ, you were unjustified; but
none want that, who consenteth to his covenant as
before; and that consent you cannot deny. Will you
live like a forsaken orphan exposed in a wilderness,
while God's tender love is saving you, and Christ is
glorying in you as the fruit of his blood, and the angels of God are serving you, and rejoicing at your
conversion? I entreat you think whether it be not
the great work that God hath called you to, to ho-

nour his grace, and propagate to all about you, as
you are able, a joyful, thankful, hoping and praising
frame of soul ; and to stir up all to the delightful
praise of God ?   As ministers must do it by preaching, all must do it by conference and example.   And
is your dejected sadness the performance of this ?"

7. When she desired to be prayed for, she wrote
down this answer which I find now in her papers.

" It is well if you know what prayer to put up, or
what to desire; I will pray for you according to the
best of my judgment ; and I will tell you for what,
that you may know what to pray for for yourself :   '
First, I will pray that your thoughts may be turned
to the magnifying of God's love; and you may remember that he is as *good* as he is *great ;* and that
you may be more sensible of his mercy, than of your
own unworthiness.   2. I will pray that you may
have so lively an apprehension of your everlasting felicity, as may make you long to be with Christ.   3.
That you may have more self-denial, and that humility which makes you little in your own eyes.   4.
That you may be much less tender, and liable to com-
motion and disquiet of mind, and less sensible of unkindnesses, and of bodily dangers, yea, and of sin
itself, while the sense of it hinders the sense of mercy.   A meek, and a quiet, and patient spirit, is of
great price in the sight of God.   I will pray that
you may be delivered from too much inward passion,
of fear, grief, or discontent.   5. I will pray, that no
creature may seem greater, better, or more regardable, or necessary to you than it is ; and that you
would look on all as walking shadows, vanity and

liars (that is, *untrusty*), further than you can see God
in them, or they lead you up to him ; that they may
never be over-loved, over-feared, over-trusted, or
their thoughts too much regarded. 6. Above all, I
will pray that you may be less *self-willed*, and not to
be too passionately or unmoveably set upon the fulfilling of all your will ; but may have a will that is
compliant with the will of God, and can change as
he would have it ; and will follow him, and not run
before him ; and can endure to be crossed and denied
by God and man, without discomposedness, and impatient trouble of mind. 7. I shall pray, that seeming wisdom may not entangle you, either in the concealment of any thing which greatly needeth your
friends' advice, or in the hiding of your talents by
unprofitable silence, as to all good discourse, upon
the enmity which you have to hypocrisy ; and that
you will not live in sins of omission, for fear of
seeming better than you are. By this you may
know wherein I think you faulty."

8. The next I find, is this advice against her resolution to go to London.

"It is not lawful to speak an idle word, and especially deliberately ; much less to go an idle journey.
What if you fall sick by the way, or some weakness
take you there, will not conscience ask you, who
called you hither ? Your weakness of spirit that
cannot endure this or that, at home, with your dearest friends, is so far below the quiet, composed forti-
tude which you should have, that you ought not to
give way to it. If you are at the command of your
impatience, how are you obedient to the command

of God? It is a greater work to bring your mind and will to the will of God, than to change place or apparel, or run away as *Jonah* in discontent. O for a mind and will that needed no more to quiet it, than to know what is the will of God, and our duty; and in every state therewith to be content. When you know your duty, do it resolutely and cheerfully, and scorn to run away, and turn your back, that you may do it without censure where you are unknown. Use well the means God here vouchsafes you, and do your duty with a quiet mind, and *follow God* in your removes."

9. Much more of such counsels she transcribed, but I forbear reciting more. She ends those papers with these words:

" The best creature-affections have a mixture of creature-imperfections, and therefore need some gall to wean us from the faulty part : God must be known to be God, our rest, and therefore the best creature to be but a creature! O miserable world! (how long must I continue in it? and why is this wretched heart so loath to leave it?) where we can have no fire without smoke, and our dearest friends must be our greatest grief; and when we begin in hope, and love, and joy, before we are aware, we fall into an answerable measure of distress. Learn by experience, when any condition is inordinately or excessively sweet to thee, to say, *From hence must be my sorrow.* (O how true!)"

CHAP. V.

Her Temper, occasioning these Troubles of Mind.

1. THE soul while in the body, works much according to the body's disposition. 1. She was of an extraordinary sharp and piercing wit.* 2. She had a natural reservedness and secresy, increased by thinking it necessary prudence not to be open; by which means she was oft misunderstood by her nearest friends, and consequently often crossed and disappointed by those that would have pleased her. And as she could understand men much by their looks and hints, so she expected all should know her mind without her expressing it, which bred her frustrations and discontents. 3. And she had a natural tenderness, and troubledness of mind, upon the crossing of her just desires; too quick, and ungovernable a sense of displeasing words or deeds. 4. She had a diseased, irresistible fearfulness; her quick, and too sensible nature was over-timorous; and to increase it, she said she was four times, before I knew her, in danger of death (of which, one was by the small pox): and more to increase it, her mother's house *(Appley Castle*, near *Wellington)*, being a garrison, it

---

* This observation is confirmed by the opinion of that great and good man, the Rev. John Howe. He says (speaking of Mrs. Baxter), 'I had the opportunity by an occasional abode some days under the same roof, several years before she came into that relation wherein she finished her course, *to observe her strangely vivid wit*, and very sober conversation.' Funeral Sermon for Mrs. Baxter.

was stormed while she was in it, and part of the housing about it burnt, and men lay killed before her face, and all of them threatened, and stripped of their clothing, so that they were fain to borrow clothes. 5. And the great work upon her soul, in her conversion, moved all her passions. 6. And then her dangerous sickness, and the sentence of death to so young a convert, must needs be a very awakening thing; and coming on her before she had any assurance of her justification, did increase her fear. 7. And in this case she lived in the churchyard side, where she saw all the burials of the dead, and kept a death's head (a skull) in her closet still before her. And other such mortifying spectacles increased her sad disposition.

2. And the excessive love which she had to her mother, did much increase her grief when she expected death.

3. Though she called it melancholy, that by all this she was cast into, yet it rather seemed a partly natural, and partly an adventitious, diseased fearfulness in a tender, over-passionate nature, that had no power to quiet her own fears, without any other cloud on her understanding.

4. And all was much increased by her wisdom, so stifling all the appearances of it, that it all inwardly wrought, and had no ease by vent.

5. And having keen spirits, and thin sharp blood, she had a strong *hemicrania* or head-ach once a month, and oft once a fortnight, or more, from the age of fifteen or sixteen years. All these together much tended to hinder her from a quiet and comfortable temper.

6. And in a word, all the operations of her soul

were very intense and strong ; strong wit, and strong love, and strong displeasure. And when God shewed her what *holiness* was, she thought she must presently have it in so great a degree as the ripest saints do here attain ; and that because she had not as much heavenly life, and sense, and delight in God as she knew she should have, and desired, she concluded that she had none that was sincere.

7. One of the first things by which her change was discovered to her mother and friends, was her fervent secret prayers : for living in a great house, of which the middle part was ruined in the wars, she chose a closet in the further end, where she thought none heard her : but some that overheard her, said, they never heard so fervent prayers from any person.

8. Yet she desired me to draw up a form suited to her own condition ; which I did, and find it now reserved among her papers ; but I cannot tell whether she ever used it, having affections and freedom of expression without it. I had thought to have annexed it for the use of afflicted penitents ; but it will be but a digression in this narrative.

CHAP. VI.

Of our Marriage, and our Habitations.

1. THE unsuitableness of our age, and my former known purposes against marriage, and against the conveniency of ministers' marriage, who have no sort of necessity, made our marriage the matter of much public talk and wonder : and the true opening of her case and mine, and the many strange occurrences which brought it to pass, would take away the won-

D

der of her friends and mine that knew us ; and the notice of it would much conduce to the understanding of some other passages of our lives : yet wise friends, by whom I am advised, think it better to omit such personal particularities, at least at this time. Both in her case and mine, there was much extraordinary, which it doth not much concern the world to be acquainted with. From the first thoughts of it, many changes and stoppages intervened, and long delays, till I was silenced and ejected with many hundreds more ; and so being separated from my old pastoral charge, which was enough to take up all my time and labour, some of my dissuading reasons were then over. And at last, on *September* 10, 1662, we were married in *Bennet-Fink* church by *Mr. Samuel Clarke,** (yet living), having been before contracted by *Mr. Simeon Ash,*† both

---

* Mr. Samuel Clarke had been a useful preacher many years in Cheshire and Warwickshire, where he had met with trouble on account of the *Et cetera* oath, &c. before he came to London ; but he here lived comfortably and usefully, holding the living of St. Bennet Fink, till ejected therefrom by the Act of Uniformity. He was one of the Commissioners at the Treaty at the Savoy. He was born Oct. 10, 1599, and died Dec. 25, 1682.

† We have the following account of this excellent divine given us by Mr. Baxter :—' Good old Mr. Simeon Ash was buried the very eve of Bartholomew day, and went seasonably to heaven at the very time when he was to be cast out of the church. He was a Christian of the primitive simplicity ; not much for controversy, nor inclined to disputes, but of a holy life and peaceful mind, and of a fluent elegancy in prayer, full of matter and excellent words. His ordinary speech was holy and edifying. Being confined much to his house by the gout, and having a good estate and a good wife,

in the presence of *Mr. Henry Ashhurst** and *Mrs. Ash.*

2. She consented to these conditions of our marriage: 1. That I would have nothing that before our

---

inclined to entertainment and liberality, his house was very much frequented by ministers. He was always cheerful, without profuse laughter, or liberty, or vain words: never troubled with doubtings of his interest in Christ, but tasting the continual love of God, was much disposed to the communicating of it to others, and comforting dejected souls. His eminent serenity made him exceedingly loved and honoured. Having preached his lecture in Cornhill, being heated, he took cold in the vestry, and thinking it would have proved but one of his old fits of the gout, he went to Highgate, but it turned to a fever. He died as he lived, in great consolation and cheerful exercise of faith, greatly encouraging all about him with joyful expressions in respect of death, and his approaching change. As soon as I came to him, gladness so excited his spirits, that he spake joyfully and full of his going to God to all about him. I staid with him his last evening, and in the night he departed.'

* Alderman Henry Ashhurst was the intimate friend of Mr. Baxter for many years, whom he held in the highest esteem. He was commonly taken for the most exemplary Christian in his time, that was of public note in the city of London. He was sound in judgment, of such admirable meekness, patience, universal charity and all good works, that his equal was rarely to be found. A volume might be written in praise of his excellent deeds, both at home and abroad; for he did not confine his charity to England, Ireland and Scotland, but extended his views in doing good to heathen lands, and was a chief instrument in the setting up a printing-press, and procuring the Bible to be translated into the Indian tongue, as well as many other good books, for the use of the heathen. He was a mere Bible Christian of the primitive stamp: no learning signified much with him, but what helped him to understand the Scriptures; and he loved no preaching so well as that which made much and pertinent use of Scripture, by clear exposition and suitable application. He liked not that which Dr. Man-

marriage was hers; that I (who wanted no outward supplies) might not seem to marry her for covetousness. 2. That she would so alter her affairs, that I might be entangled in no law-suits. 3. That she would expect none of my time which my ministerial work should require.

3. When we were married, her sadness and melancholy vanished; counsel did something to it, and contentment something; and being taken up with our household affairs, did somewhat. And we lived in inviolated love, and mutual complacency, sensible of the benefit of mutual help. These near nineteen years I know not that ever we had any breach in point of love, or point of interest, save only that she somewhat grudged that I had persuaded her for my

---

ton was wont to call *gentleman-preaching*, set out with fine things, and laced and gilded, plainly speaking, *self-preaching, man-pleasing* and *pride*. He was esteemed, loved and honoured, both at home and abroad, by his children, servants, neighbours and fellow-citizens. And if you would truly know what was the meritorious cause of all this love and honour, says Mr. Baxter, I will tell you, *It was the image of Christ* and the fruits of his holy doctrine and his Spirit. Though he was such a holy man, and of a strong body, it pleased God to try his patience by a very painful disease, which he endured for many years; but at last, in extremity of torment he underwent an operation, and after much suffering and patience died in great peace and quietness of mind, and thus suddenly passed from the exercise of faith and patience, into sight and rest. His last words, (save his farewel, and ' Come Lord Jesus,') were to an old friend, ' *To walk in the way of God, will be comfort at death.*' It was commonly said by magistrates, ministers and people, that ' We have lost the most excellent pattern of piety, charity and all virtue that this city hath bred in our times.' And to what other end, concludes Mr. Baxter, have I said all this of him? In general, ' Go thou and do likewise.'

quietness to surrender so much of her estate, to a disabling her from helping others so much as she earnestly desired.

4. But that even this was not from a covetous mind, is evident by these instances. (1.) Though her portion, which was £2000, besides that given up aforesaid, was, by ill debtors, £200 lost in her mother's time, and £200 after, before her marriage; and all she had reduced to almost £1650, yet she never grudged at any thing that the poverty of debtors deprived her of.

(2.) She had before been acquainted with the Lord Chancellor's offering me a bishopric; and though it might have taken off the censure of those relations that thought she debased herself in marrying me, and also might have seemed desirable to her for the wealth as well as the honour, she was so far from desiring my accepting it, that I am persuaded had I done it, it would have alienated her much from me in point of esteem and love. Not that she had any opinion against episcopacy then, that ever I could perceive, but that she abhorred a worldly, mercenary mind in a minister of Christ, and was a sharp censurer of all that for gain, or honour, or worldly ends, would stretch their consciences to any thing that they thought God forbade. And I am assured (though towards her end she wished she had been more able to relieve the needy, and do more good; yet) she lived a far more contented life in our mean condition, even when she stooped to receive from others that had been strangers to her, than she would have done had I been a bishop, and she had had many thousand pounds more at her disposal; yea, I am persuaded she would not easily have endured it.

(3.) Another trial of her as to wealth and honour, was when I, and all such others, were cast out of all possession and hope of all ecclesiastical maintenance; she was not ignorant of the scorn and the jealousies, and wrath and prosecutions that I was like to be exposed to; yea, she had heard and seen it already begun by bishop *Morley*'s forbidding me to preach before, and preaching himself, and his dean, and many others, fiercely against me in *Kidderminster* pulpit; she had quickly heard them that were cast out and silenced, deeply accused as if they had deserved it. To choose a participation of such a life that had no encouragement from any worldly wealth or honour, yea, that was exposed to such certain suffering which had no end in prospect on this side death, did shew that she was far from covetousness. Much more evidence of this I shall shew you as it falls in its place.

5. Among other troubles that her marriage exposed her to, one was our oft necessitated removals; which to those that must take houses, and bind themselves to landlords, and fit and furnish them, is more than for single persons that have no such clogs or cares. First, we took a house in *Moorfields*, after at *Acton*; next that, another at *Acton*; and after that, another there; and after that, we were put to remove to one of the former again; and after that, to divers others in another place and county, as followeth; and the women have most of that sort of trouble. But she easily bore it all.

And I know not that ever she came to any place where she did not extraordinarily win the love of the inhabitants (unless in any street where she staid so short a time, as not to be known to them). Had she

had but the riches of the world to have done the
good that she had a heart to do, how much would
she have been loved, who in her mean and low condition won so much!

And her carriage won more love than her liberality; she could not endure to hear one give another
any sour, rough, or hasty word; her speech and countenance was always kind and civil, whether she had
any thing to give or not.

And all her kindness tended to some better end,
than barely to relieve people's bodily wants; even to
oblige them to some duty that tended to the good of
their souls, or to deliver them from some straits
which filled them with hurtful care, and became a
matter of great temptation to them. If she could
hire the poor to hear God's word, from Conformist
or Nonconformist, or to read good, serious, practical
books, whether written by Conformists or Nonconformists, it answered her end and desire : and many
an hundred books hath she given to those ends.
But of these things more hereafter. This is here
but to answer the aforesaid objection, and to lead on
to the following particular passages of her life.

6. While I was at *Acton*, her carriage and charity
so won the people there, that all that I ever heard of,
greatly esteemed and loved her. And she being earnestly desirous of doing good, prepared her house
for the reception of those that would come in, to be
instructed by me, between the morning and evening
public assemblies, and after. And the people that
had never been used to such things, accounted
worldly, ignorant persons, gave us great hopes of their
edification and reformation, and filled the room, and
went with me also into the church (which was at my

door). And when I was after removed, the people
hearing that I again wanted a house (being ten miles
off), they unanimously subscribed a request to me,
to return to my old house with them, and offered to
pay my house-rent, which I took kindly: and it was
much her winning conversation which thus won
their love.

7. When I was carried thence to the common
gaol, for teaching them, as aforesaid, I never perceived her troubled at it: she cheerfully went with me
into prison; *she brought her best bed thither*; and did
much to remove the removable inconveniences of the
prison. I think she had scarce ever a pleasanter
time in her life than while she was with me there.
And whereas people upon such occasions were not
unapt to be liberal, it was against her mind to receive more than necessity required. Only three persons gave me just as much as paid lawyers' and pri-
son-charges, and when one offered me more, she
would not receive it: but all was far short of the
great charges of our removal to another habitation.*

---

* Of the cruel treatment he met with at this time, Mr. Baxter observes, 'My imprisonment was at present no suffering to
me; for I had an honest gaoler, who shewed me all the kindness
he could. I had a large room, and the liberty of walking in a fair
garden; and my wife was never so cheerful a companion to me as in
prison, and was very much against my seeking to be released; and
she had brought so many necessaries, that we kept house as contentedly and comfortably as at home, though in a narrower room,
and I had the sight of more of my friends in a day, than I had at
home in half a year. The number of visitors by day did put me
out of hope of studying, or doing any thing but entertain them. I
had neither leave at any time to go out of doors, much less to a
church on the Lord's-day, nor on that day to have any come to
me, nor to preach to any but my own family.'

8. The parliament making a new, sharper law against us, I was forced to remove into another county; thither she went with me, and removed her goods that were moveable, from *Acton* to *Totteridge*, being engaged for the rent of the house we left. At *Totteridge*, the first year, few poor people are put to the hardness that she was put to; we could have no house but part of a poor farmer's, where the chimnies so extremely smoked, as greatly annoyed her health; for it was a very hard winter, and the coal-smoke so filled the room that we all day sat in, that it was as a cloud, and we were nearly suffocated with the stink. And she had ever a great straitness of the lungs, that could not bear smoke or closeness. This was the greatest bodily suffering that her outward condition put her to; which was increased by my continual pain there. But her charity to her poor landlady, set her son apprentice, who now liveth well

9. Thence we removed to a house, which we took to ourselves, which required so great alterations and amendment, as took her up much time and labour: and to her great comfort, she got *Mr. Corbet** and his

---

* 'Mr. John Corbet was sometime a preacher in Glocester, after at Chichester, and after that at Bramshot in Hampshire, which place he left, to keep the peace of his conscience. He was a man of extraordinary judgment, moderation, peaceable principles, and blameless life; a solid preacher, and well known by his writings. He lived peaceably in London without gathering any assembly for public preaching. Dwelling at Totteridge with Alderman Webb; his great love drew him there to be near me, says Mr. Baxter, with whom awhile he took up his habitation. God many years afflicted him with a painful disorder, which at last caused his death. While the pain was tolerable to nature he endured it, and ceased not preaching till a fortnight before he was carried up to London to

wife to dwell with us.   And in all these changes and
troubles she lived in great peace.

10. When the king's Declarations and Licenees
gave Nonconformists leave to build meeting-places,
and preach, she was against my going to *London*,
till others were there settled, lest I should anticipate
them, and gather any auditors, who would else go to
others, especially their old ejected pastors; but when
others were settled, she was earnest with me to go,
for the exercise of my ministry.

11. Upon our removal to *London*, out of tender
regard to my health, which she thought the situation
might contribute much unto, she chose and took for
us this most pleasant and convenient house in *South-
ampton-square*, where she died.   These were our removes.

CHAP. VII.

Of her exceeding desires to do good.

1. As at her conversion, and in her sickness, she ab-
solutely devoted herself and all that she had to God;
so she earnestly set herself to perform it to the last.
At first she gave but the tenth of her income to the
poor; but I quickly convinced her that God must
not be stinted, but as all was his, so all must be used
for him by his stewards, and of all we must give ac-

---

undergo an operation, but before that could be done, in a fortnight
more he died.   He had lived in my house before, and was greatly
honoured by my wife.   She got not long after his excellent, exemplary wife, (daughter to Dr. Twiss) to be her companion, but enjoyed that comfort but a little while, which I have longer enjoyed.'

count; only in his appointed order we must use it, which is, 1. For our own natural necessities. 2. For public necessary good. 3. For the necessities of our children, and such relations as are part of our charge. 4. And then for the godly poor. 5. And then for the common poor's necessities. 6. And lastly, for conveniences; but nothing for unuseful things.

2. To name the particular great instances of her private charity, is neither suitable to my ends, nor her desires. I will instance but some of her more public cares.

3. She was earnestly desirous of the winning of souls, and of the utmost improvement of mine and other men's labours to that end. At *Acton*, I told you how she promoted it; and at *Totteridge, out of church-time*, she gladly opened her doors to her neighbours, that would come in for instruction.

4. At *London*, when she saw me too dull and backward to seek any employment till I was called, and that most places in the city had some supplies; she first fished out of me in what place I most desired more preaching. I told her in *St. Martin*'s parish, where are said to be forty thousand more than can come into the church, especially among all the new buildings at *St. James*'s, where neighbours may live like Americans, and have heard no sermon of many years.

When she had once heard this, without my knowledge she sets one to seek after some capacious room there; and none was found, but divers rooms over the market-house laid together. She gets one to take them. And they two agreed to importune me to preach each morning, and in the afternoon to get by turns the ablest ministers they could procure in

London. And to that end she got a minister a hundred miles off to come up to help me, promising him £40. a year, to go from day to day to supply the places of such eminent ministers as should be got. All this charge, besides paying a clerk, and a woman to look to the seats, rose high. Part of it the people paid, and the rest she paid herself.

5. Hence God was pleased to remove us, but by the interposition of a marvellous deliverance. The roof of that market-house is a vast weight, and was ill-contrived to lie much on one beam in the middle of the floor: the place being greatly crowded, the beam gave so great a crack as put all the people in a fear. But a second crack set them all on running, and crying out at the windows for ladders; I having seen the like before at *Dunstan's, Fleet-street,** while I was preaching (which occasioned the pulling down and new building of the church), reproved them

---

* Mr. Baxter's ministry being attended by crowded congregations, a circumstance happened that drove him from his place of preaching, which was at this time that of St. Dunstan's, Fleet-street, where he was lecturer to Dr. Bates. He thus relates the occurrence in his Life; 'It fell out that at Dunstan's church in the midst of sermon, a little lime and dust, and perhaps a piece of a brick or two, fell down in the steeple or belfry near the boys, which put the whole congregation into sudden melancholy, so that they thought the steeple and church were falling; which put them all into so confused a haste to get away, that indeed the noise of the feet in the galleries sounded like the falling of the stones; so that the people crowded out of doors. The women left some of them a scarf, and some a shoe behind them, and some in the galleries cast themselves down upon those below, because they could not get down the stairs. I sat down in the pulpit, seeing and pitying their vain distemper, and as soon as I could be heard, I entreated their silence, and went on. The people were no sooner

sharply for their fears, and would have gone on to preach; but see the strange hand of God on her that set all the work on foot! After the first crack, she got down the stairs through the crowd, where others could not get that were stronger. The first man she met, she asked him what profession he was of; he said, a carpenter. Saith she, Can you suddenly put a prop under the middle of this beam? The man dwelt close by, had a meet prop ready, suddenly put it under, while all we above knew nothing of it; but the man's knocking increased the people's fears and cry. We were glad all to be gone; and the next morning took a skilful workman to take up the boards, and search the beam; which we all saw had two such rents, so long and so wide, and the sound part left was so slender, that we took it for a wonder that the house fell not suddenly.

---

quieted, and got in again, and the auditory composed, but some that stood upon a bench near the communion-table, brake the bench with their weight, so that the noise renewed their fear again, and they were worse disordered than before; so that one old woman was heard at the church door asking forgiveness of God, for not taking the first warning, and promising, if God would deliver her this once, she would take heed of coming thither again. When they were again quieted I went on.' Dr. Bates, in his funeral sermon for Mr. Baxter, represents it as a signal instance of his firm faith in the Divine Providence, that after the hurry was over, he resumed his discourse with this remarkable passage to compose the minds of the people: 'We are in the service of God, to prepare ourselves, that we may be fearless at the great noise of the dissolving world, when the heavens shall pass away, and the elements melt with fervent heat; the earth also, and the works therein shall be burnt up,' &c. The church being old, it was in great part pulled down and rebuilt; during which reparation, he preached at St. Bride's.

6. But this fright increased my wife's diseased frightfulness ; so that she never got off all the effects of it while she lived. The fear, and the marvellous deliverance, made her promise to God two things : 1. To keep the anniversary memorial of it in public thanksgiving (which she did). And 2. To build a safer place, where they might meet with less fear. And it too deeply touched her mind to think that it was she that took the place, and brought them all thither. And if eight hundred persons had been there buried in the ruins, as the Papists were at *Blackfriars,** O what a dreadful thing it would have been in the heavy loss, the many dolorous families, and the public scandal! These were too great thoughts to fall on a weak and too passionate nature.

7. According to her promise, she paid for that place, and presently set to seek and build another. And there was there no fit grounds near it to be had, but two ; of which one was in *Oxendon-street,* which she could not have without giving thirty pounds a year ground-rent, and to be at all the charge of building on it, and this but for a lease not very long. But *she must do it* by promise and desire. She gets a friend to make the bargain, takes the ground, and begs money to build on it a chapel, which tempted us by the ill advice of a friend, to take also the front ground to the street, and build two little houses on

---

* Towards the end of the reign of James I. a dreadful accident called the *Fatal Vespers* happened at Blackfriars. A celebrated preacher of the order of the Jesuits, named father Drury, gave a sermon to a large audience, in a spacious room up three pair of stairs. In the midst of the discourse the floor fell, and ninety-four persons besides the preacher perished.

it, to our great loss, all her own money, and many times more, being laid out upon them, much against her inclination.

8. When that chapel was finished, I began and preached there but one day, being to go on the morrow into the country. It unhappily fell out, that Secretary *Henry Coventry*'s house was on the back part of it, who resolved that it should not be used by us. The next Lord's-day, when I was far off, and left my wife at home, she got one *Mr. Seddon*, a Derbyshire stranger then come to town, to preach there, (an humble, pious man, that had suffered imprisonment formerly by *Cromwell*'s party for being for the King's restoration at the rising of *Sir George Booth :)* Secretary *Coventry* thinking I would be there, had got three justices with a warrant as for me, to have apprehended me, and sent me to gaol. But it fell on *Mr. Seddon*. But because the warrant made for me, was so altered as to the name that it suited not his case, after some time of imprisonment he had his *Habeas Corpus*, and by the justice of worthy Judge *Hale*** and

---

* Sir Matthew Hale was born in Aldersley, in Gloucestershire, in 1600. He was a very learned man, a sound lawyer, an upright judge, and an exemplary Christian. Of this excellent man Mr. Baxter gives the following account. 'The last year of my abode at Acton, I had the happiness of a neighbour whom I cannot easily praise above his worth, which was Sir Matthew Hale, lord chief justice of the Exchequer, whom all the judges and lawyers of England admired for his skill in law, and for his justice; and scholars honoured for his learning, and I highly valued for his sincerity, mortification, self-denial, humility, conscientiousness and his close fidelity in friendship. Soon after he came to town I had notice of his desire of my acquaintance; and I scarcely ever conversed so profitably with any other person in my life. Falling into a languishing disease from which he was not likely to recover, resolvedly

other judges, was delivered. But he was a tender man, and my wife sensible that she was the occasion (which did her no good), and all the burden lay on

---

petitioned for his dismission and gave up his place, having gone through his employments, and gone off the stage with more universal love and honour for his skill, wisdom, piety and resolved justice, than ever I heard or read that any Englishman ever did before him, or any magistrate in the world of his rank, since the days of the kings of Israel. He resolved, in his weakness, that the place should not be a burden to him, nor he to it. And after all his great practice and places, he tells me, that with his own inheritance and all he is not now worth £500 per Annum; so little sought he after gain. He may most truly be called, the pillar and basis, or ground of justice, as Paul called (not the church, but) Timothy (in the church) the pillar and basis of truth. His digested knowledge of law above all men, and next in philosophy, and much in theology, was very great; his sincere honesty and humility admirable; his garb, and house, and attendance so very mean and low, and he so resolutely avoided all the diversions and vanities of the world, that he was herein the marvel of his age. Some made it a scandal, but his wisdom chose it for his convenience, that in his age he married a woman of no estate, suitable to his disposition, to be to him as a nurse. He succeeded me in one of the meanest houses that ever I had lived in, and there hath ever since continued with full content, till now that he is going to his native country, in all likelihood to die there. It is not the least of my pleasure that I have lived some years in his more than ordinary love and friendship, and that we are now waiting which shall be first in heaven; whither, he saith, he is going with full content and acquiescence in the will of a gracious God, and doubts not but we shall shortly live together. O what a blessed world were this, were the generality of magistrates such as he!' A few days before his death, which took place in 1675, he went into the churchyard of Aldersley, and there chose his grave. The best known of his writings, which are numerous, are, 'The Primitive Organization of Mankind, considered and explained according to the Light of Nature,r &c. folio; 'The History of the Pleas of the Crown,' folio; 'Contemplations, Moral and Divine,' 3 vols. 8vo.

her to maintain him, to visit and comfort him, to pay the lawyers, and discharge all fees; which as I remember cost her £20; and yet we were calumniated as if I (that was twenty miles off) had put another to suffer in my stead.

9. When she saw that we could not be suffered to preach in the place which upon her promise she had built; she was very glad that *Dr. Lloyd* and the parishioners accepted of it for their public worship; asking them no more rent than we were to pay for the ground, and the room over for a vestry at £5, and asking no advantage for all the money laid out on the building: yet since, the purchase of the fee-simple of the chapel-ground hath cost me £200 more, and the adjoining ground £200 more, to my great loss.

10. So much was her heart set on the helping the ignorant, untaught poor about *St. James's*, that she set up a school there to teach some poor children to read, and the Catechism freely; and thereby also relieved a poor honest man that taught them, who hath a wife and many children, and no other maintenance of his own, *Mr. Bruce*. And she would fain have set up more, had she had money; for this she begged awhile of her good friends; but they quickly gave over; and she paid him mostly of her own, £6 a year, till her death. I mention this, to move some charitable people to continue it; and to tell them, that in the many great out-parishes of *London*, there are multitudes of the children of the poor, that spend their time in idleness and play, and are never taught to read; and that there are many good women very poor, that would be glad of a small stipend to teach such to read, and the Catechism; and so both might

have relief and help; and I think charity can scarce
be better used, as honest *Mr. Gouge** hath in *Wales*
found by experience. And I would such places in

---

* Thomas Gouge, minister of St. Sepulchre's church in London,
from which he was ejected in 1662 for nonconformity, was the son
of the eminent Dr. William Gouge of Blackfriars. He was a man
of exemplary piety, charity, humility, sincerity and moderation.
Mr. Baxter says, ' I never heard any one person, of what rank,
sort or sect soever, speak one word to his dishonour, or name
any fault that ever they charged on his life or doctrine.'
He was once possessed of a good estate; but when he had
lost much by the Fire (1666), had settled his children, and had
his wife taken from him by death, he had but £150 a year left:
and he gave one hundred of it to charitable uses. It was his daily
work to do all the good he could, with as great diligence and constancy as other men labour at their trades. He visited the poor,
and stirred up the rich, in whom he had any interest, to devote at
least a tenth part of their estates to works of charity. He was the
founder and supporter of above three hundred schools in the chief
towns of Wales, for the propagation of useful knowledge; and when
between sixty and seventy years of age he used to travel yearly
through the country and disperse what money he could spare himself or collect from others among the poor, labouring, persecuted
ministers there. He preached himself in Wales, till they drove
him from the place by persecution. He went constantly to the parish
churches, and sometimes communicated with them, and was au-
thorised by an old University licence to preach occasionally, and
yet for so doing was excommunicated even in Wales, and that
while he was doing all this good. He procured a very fair impres-
sion of the Bible in the Welch tongue, to the number of eight
thousand; one thousand of which were freely given to the poor, and
the rest sent to the principal cities and towns in Wales, to be sold
to the rich at reasonable rates. He was used to say often with
pleasure, That he had two livings, which he would not exchange
for two of the greatest in England, meaning Wales, where he used
to travel every year to spread knowledge, piety and charity; and

London where the tenth or the fourth person in the parish cannot come to church, and many thousands have disused themselves from God's public worship, and breed up their children accordingly, were pitied as well as *Wales*.

11. When she saw that I could not use the chapel which she built, she presently hired another near (ready built, for gain) in *Swallow-street*, that the poor people where I had begun (through God's mercy with considerable success) might still be taught: and when I had there awhile continued, and was kept out, by the officers' standing at the door with the justices' warrants, many months together, it was her care and act to refer it to many good ministers, to choose one for the place that would be better endured by them that would not endure me; and a faithful, painful, self-denying man was chosen, who hath there done much good, and still doth.

12. When I was thence driven, it was her choice that I should go quite to *Southwark* each Lord's-day, to preach to a congregation of poor people there.

Christ's Hospital, where he used freely to catechise the poor children, in order to the well laying the foundation of religion in them in their tender years. He likewise caused to be translated and printed in Welch, The Church Catechism, with a Practical Exposition;—The Book of Common Prayer;—The Whole Duty of Man;—The Practice of Piety, and other practical books. Mr. Gouge died suddenly in 1681, in the 77th year of his age, without any sickness, or pain, or fear of death; he was heard to give a groan in his sleep and he was gone. Dr. Tillotson, who preached his funeral sermon, ascribes to him the first foundation of that charitable design of employing the poor at work, which Mr. Thomas Firmin afterwards improved, and which met with such general applause. His works, though few, are valuable.

13. When *Dr. Manton's* place at *Covent Garden* was void, it was her desire that I should preach once a day there, because being near, many of the poor of *St. James's* would come thither, as they did.

14. She got from her friends also money to help to build another very useful chapel for another, among a numerous poor people, where still much good is done. And she promoted two or three such more.

15. She was very impatient of public collections for the ministers, or for the rent of the place, because it sounded ill, and prejudiced the ignorant and covetous, and troubled the poor that had no money; and therefore did the utmost she could with her own purse and her friends' to avoid it, knowing that rent must be paid, and ministers and their families must have bread, and it is a pity that they should be under the cares of want.

16. She was so far from crossing me in my preaching freely without salary, or gathering a church that would maintain me, or making collections, or getting subscriptions, that she would not have endured any such thing if I had desired it; though she knew that the labourer was worthy of his hire, and that God had ordained, that they that preach the Gospel should live of the Gospel: yet she knew that all must be done to the furtherance of the Gospel, and to edifying; and was of *Paul's* mind, that would rather die, than any should make his glorying void, and deprive him of that reward. Therefore it was so far from offending her (as it would be with many ministers' wives that were in want, and might have such maintenance as is their due), that I neither conformed, nor took any place of gain, that it was a

much by her will as my own, that for the first nine
or ten years of my ejected state I took not so much
as any private gift to supply my wants, except £10
a year from *Sergeant Fountaine*,* which his importunity, and my civility would not permit me to refuse.

17. And I take it yet for a greater part of her self-
denial and charity, that when her own estate proved
much too short to maintain her in the exercise of
such good works as she was devoted to, she at length
refused not to accept with thanks the liberality of
others, and to live partly on charity, that she might
exercise charity to them that could not so easily get
it from others as we could do; and accordingly of
latter years, divers faithful, pious friends (no way re-
lated to us, or obliged by us) have been so free, kind
and liberal, that I have much ado to forbear here

---

* Of this excellent man, Mr. Baxter thus speaks: 'This year
died Sergeant John Fountaine, the only person from whom I received an annual sum of money; which through God's mercy I
needed not, yet I could not in civility refuse. He gave me ten
pounds a year from the time of my silencing till his death. I was a
stranger to him before the king's return; save that when he was
judge (before he was one of the keepers of the great seal) he did
our country great service against vice. He was a man of a sound
and quick understanding, an upright, impartial mind and life, of too
much testiness in his weakness; but of a most believing, serious fer-
vency towards God, and open, zealous owning of true piety and
holiness, without owning the little partialities of sects as most men
that ever I came near in his sickness. When he lay sick, which
was almost a year, he sent to the judges and lawyers that sent to
visit him, such answers as these:—I thank your lord or master
for his kindness; present my service to him, and tell him it is a
great work to die well; his time is near; all worldly glory must
come down; entreat him to keep his integrity, overcome temptation, please God, and prepare to die.'

naming them, in expression of their bounty and my
thanks. And I must say of her, that once her pride
would not have stooped to be so much beholden, as
to live on the charity of strangers.

18. When warrants were out (from *Sir Thomas
Davis*) to distrain of my goods for fines for my
preaching, she did, without any repining, encourage
me to undergo the loss, and did herself take the trouble of removing and hiding my library awhile, (many
scores being so lost,) and after to give it away, *bona
fide*, some to *New England*, and the most at home, to
avoid distraining on them. And the danger of imprisonment, and paying £40 for every sermon, was
so far from inclining her to hinder or discourage me
from any one sermon, that if she did but think I had
the least fear, or self-saving by fleshly wisdom, in
shrinking from my undertaken office-work, it was so
great a trouble to her, that she could not hide it,
who could too much hide many others.

19. She was exceeding impatient with any non-
conforming ministers that shrunk for fear of suffering, or that were over-querulous and sensible of their
wants or dangers; and would have no man be a minister that had not so much self-denial as to lay down
all at the feet of Christ, and count no cost or suffering too dear to serve him. She greatly hated choos-
ing or using the sacred ministry for wealth, ease, or
honour, or any worldly end, serving the flesh under
the name of serving Christ, and looking to be reve-
renced and honoured in this taking of God's name in
vain.

20. Accordingly after some years, wherein a larger
course had been taken, she was against my persuad-
ing parents to devote their children to the ministr

that had but good wits and parts, and were not profane, though my success with some did much encourage me to it heretofore : but her sense of the sin
and mischief of bad ministers, made her persuade all,
that in that case she had to do with, to take heed of
devoting their sons to the ministry, till they had
good reason to judge them truly godly ; and as she
would not have pious persons to marry such as were
not pious, on pretence of hopes that God would convert them ; so much less would she have such hopes
that have no promise from God, pretended for devoting unsanctified lads to the sacred office : she saw
how many, even of good men's children, profaned
the ministry, and turned to any course that did but
serve their worldly interest ; that she was vehemently
against addicting any to that office, that had not besides good wits and parts, so great a love to God and
souls, as to come to it with absolute self-denial, resolved to serve Christ at the dearest rates, and take
his acceptance, and the winning of souls for their benefice.

She was not willing to entice any into the way of
the ministry, as a common trade to live by in the
world ; and would have had two or three reading,
writing, and catechising schools set up, instead of one
grammar-school : and she would not have parents
make *scholars* of bad children, nor send them to the
Universities, lest when they had a little wordy learning they should make themselves ministers, whether
their parents would or not ; and so a swarm of such
as had been a few years at the University, should
think a benefice their due, and take the charge of the
souls of many, that never knew the worth of one,
nor how it must be qualified or guided.

21. Her expectations of liberality to the poor
from others were too high, and her displeasure too
great towards them that denied her; whereupon
when she saw a worthy person in debt, or prison, or
in great want, she would promise to gather them such
a sum, and sometimes she was put to pay most of it
herself.   But a fortnight or month before she died,
she promised to get £20, towards the relief of one of
known name and worth, and could get but £8, and
somewhat over of it, and paid all the rest herself.

22. Her judgment was, that we ought to give
more or less to every one that asketh, if we have it;
and that *neighbourhood,* and *notice,* and *asking,* next
to *known indigence,* and *great worth,* are the marks by
which to know to whom God would have us give.   I
thought, that besides these, we must exercise prudence in discerning the degrees of need and worth.
But she practised as she thought, and especially to
them in prison for debt; and blamed me if I denied
any one.

23. Alas! I know many poor widows, and others,
that think they have now lost a mother, and are left
desolate, whom I could wish some that are able
would help, instead of the help which they have lost.

24. She was much more liberal to many of my
own poor kindred than I was: but her way was not
to maintain them in idleness, but to take children,
and set them to some trade, or help them out of
some special straits.

25. To her own kindred she bare a most tender
love: but her care was most to get them to be good,
and save their souls, and next to settle them well in
the world.   I had ever been greatly averse to motion
marriages, yet she even compelled me (first satisfy-

ing my reason) to be a motioner of a wife to her only
brother's son, who, it is said, was worth to him
above £20,000. And her sister's children she loved
as if they had been her own, especially three daugh-
ters.

26. There are some things charged on her as
faults, which I shall mention. 1. That she busied
her head so much about churches, and works of charity, and was not content to live privately and quietly. But this is but what profane unbelievers say
against all zeal and serious godliness; *What needs
there all this ado?* Doth not *Paul* call some women
his helps in the Gospel? He that knows what it is
to do good, and makes it the business of his life in
the world, and knows what it is to give account of
our stewardship, and to be doomed as the unprofitable, slothful servant, will know how to answer this
accusation.

27. Another accusation is, that she was wasteful,
and imprudent in leaving me so much in debt.
To that I answer, (1.) Let any one that reads what
went before, consider what she did, and he will not
wonder at her debts : it was not to pamper her own
body; she used mean clothing, and a far meaner
diet for her own person, I think much less than *Cor-
naro*'s and *Lessius*'s proportion.

(2.) And she went into no debt but (by mortgage or
otherwise) she gave the creditors good security for.

(3.) But I confess she and I differed in this; I
thought I was to give but all my income, and not to
borrow to give, unless in some public, or extraordinary case : she thought otherwise, that while she
could give security, she ought to borrow to relieve

E

the poor, especially the most worthy. Nor did she draw upon us any debt, but what there was not only sufficient security for, but also a fair prospect of ourselves having a competency left, had it pleased God to lengthen her life ; and I am far from fearing want myself.

But so much for opening the course of her studies, labours, expenses, and indeed her delights.

CHAP. VIII.

Of her Mental Qualifications, and her Infirmities.

1. I DOUBT not but some of these accusers will say, *Why open you all this? Were not you the master? and do not you hereby praise yourself; or else confess that she was your governess?*

Answ. (1.) Perhaps love and grief may make me speak more than many will think fit. But though some passion blind the judgment, some doth but suscitate it to duty; and God made it to that end : and I will not be judged by any that never felt the like.

(2.) Did not Christ say of *Mary's* box of ointment, that it should be remembered wherever that Gospel was preached? And was it not *Judas* that said, *What need this waste?* And were not the poor's clothing, made by *Dorcas*, shewed to move *Peter?* The poor we have always with us. Do the covetous believe, that what we do to his people, we do to Christ?

(3.) It was not mine which she gave, but her own, that I am now mentioning, and what she procured.

(4.) But I am not ashamed to have been much ruled by her prudent love in many things. And you will the less wonder when I have told you what she and I were.

2. For myself, my constant pains, and weakness, and ministerial labours, forbade me the care of outward things. I had never much known worldly cares : before I was married I had no need ; afterwards she took the care on her; and disuse had made it intolerable to me. I feel now more of it than ever I did, when yet I have so little a way to go.

3. And as for her (I speak the truth), her apprehension of such things was so much quicker, and more discerning than mine, that though I was naturally somewhat tenacious of my own conceptions, her reasons, and my experience usually told me, that she was in the right, and knew more than I. She would at the first hearing understand the matter better than I could do by many and long thoughts.

4. And the excellency of her reason lay not so much in the speculative, as the *prudential, practical part:* I must say, that in this I never knew her equal. In very hard cases about what was to be done, she would suddenly open all the way that was to be opened, in things of the family, estate, or any civil business. And to confess the truth, experience acquainted her, that I knew less in such things than she; and therefore was willing she should take it all upon her.

5. Yea, I will say that, which they that believe me to be no liar, will wonder at; *Except in cases that require learning, and skill in theological difficulties, she was better at resolving a case of conscience than most*

divines that ever I knew in all my life. I often put cases to her, which she suddenly so resolved, as to convince me of some degree of oversight in my own resolution. Insomuch that of late years, I confess, that I was used to put all, save secret cases, to her, and hear what she could say. Abundance of difficulties were brought me, some about restitution, some about injuries, some about references, some about vows, some about marriage promises, and many such like; and she would lay all the circumstances presently together, compare them, and give me a more exact resolution than I could do.

6. As to religion, we were so perfectly of one mind, that I know not that she differed from me in any one point, or scarce a circumstance, except in the prudential management of what we were agreed in. She was for universal love of all true Christians, and against appropriating the church to a party, and against censoriousness and partiality in religion; she was for acknowledging all that is of God in Conformists and Nonconformists: but she had much more reverence for the elder Conformists than for most of the young ones, who ventured upon things which Dissenters had so much to say against, without weighing, or understanding the reasons on both sides, merely following others for worldly ends, without a tender fear of sinning; especially if any young men of her own friends were inclined merely to swim with the stream, without due trial of the case, it greatly displeased her, and she thought hardly of them.

7. She had in her youth been tempted to doubt of the life to come, and of the truth of the Scripture; but she was so fully resolved and settled herein, tha

her confident assurance of it was the life of all her life and practice.

8. After all the doubts of her sincerity and salvation, and all the fears and sadness thereupon, which cast her into melancholy, she so far overcame them all, that for near these nineteen years that I have lived with her, I think I never heard her thrice speak a doubting word of her salvation, but oft of her hopeful persuasions, that we should live together in heaven. It being my judgment and constant practice, to make those that I teach, understand, that the Gospel is glad tidings of great joy; and that holiness lies especially in delighting in God, his word and works; and in his joyful praise, and hopes of glory; and longing for, and seeking the heavenly Jerusalem; and living as fruitfully to the church and others, as we can do in the world: and that this must be wrought by the most believing apprehensions of God's goodness, as equal to his greatness, and of his great love to mankind manifested in our redemption, and by believing the grace and riches of Christ, and the comforting office of the Holy Ghost, and studying daily God's promises and mercies, and our everlasting joys. And that religion consists in doing God's commanding will, and quietly and joyfully trusting and resting in his promising and disposing will. And that fear and sorrow are but to remove impediments, and further all this.

And this doctrine by degrees she drunk in, and so fully consented to, that (though timorousness was her disease) her judgment was quieted and settled herein.

9. The nature of true religion, holiness, obedience, and all duty to God and man, was printed in her conceptions in so distinct and clear a character, as

made her endeavours and expectations still look at greater exactness, than I and such as I could reach. She was very desirous that we should all have lived in a constancy of devotion, and a blameless innocency: and in this respect she was the meetest helper that I could have had in the world (that ever I was acquainted with): for I was apt to be over-careless in my speech, and too backward to my duty; and she was still endeavouring to bring me to greater wariness and strictness in both. If I spake rashly or sharply, it offended her: if I carried it (as I was apt) with too much neglect of ceremony, or humble compliment to any, she would modestly tell me of it: if my very looks seemed not pleasant, she would have had me amend them (which my weak, pained state of body indisposed me to do). If I forgat any week to catechise my servants, and familiarly instruct them personally (besides my ordinary family-duties), she was troubled at my remissness. And whereas of late years my decay of spirits, and diseased heaviness and pain, made me much more seldom and cold in profitable conference and discourse in my house, than I had been when I was younger, and had more ease, and spirits, and natural vigour, she much blamed me, and was troubled at it, as a wrong to herself and others. Though yet her judgment agreed with mine, that too much and often table-talk of the best things, doth but tend to dull the common hearers, and harden them under it as a customary thing: and that too much good talk may bring it into contempt, or make it ineffectual.

And of late years, my constant weakness and pain made me unable to speak much in my ordinary course of duty; and my writings, preachings and other public duty (which I ever thought I was bound to prefer before lesser) did so wholly take up those few hours of the day, which I had out of my bed, that I was seldomer in secret prayer with my wife than she desired.

10. Indeed it troubleth me to think how oft I told her, that I never understood *Solomon's* words, *Eccles. vii. 16,* but by the exposition of her case; *Be not righteous overmuch, neither make thyself over-wise: why shouldst thou destroy thyself?* I doubt not but *Solomon* spake of *human, civil righteousness and wisdom, as a means respecting temporal prosperity or adversity,* rather than spiritual, holy righteousness, respecting God's everlasting reward : or if it were extended to religious righteousness, it can be but against superstition, falsely called *righteousness.*

But as to our present case, I must thus resolve the question, *Whether one can be religiously wise and righteous overmuch ?* And I answer, That we must distinguish between, 1. *Material and formal righteousness.* 2. *Between objective and subjective measures of it.* *Of the good and bad consequents and effects.* And 1. No man can be *formally* and properly too wise or too *righteous.* Else it would charge God with error ; for formal, proper righteousness is nothing but our conformity to God's governing will. And if our obedience were too much, and to be blamed, God's commands were to be blamed, that required it. But very strict actions are commonly called *righteousness,* as a written prayer or words are called a prayer, though properly wanting the form, it is not so. And not only a good object, but a right end, principle, and mode, and circumstances, go to make an action righteous. 2. That action which compared with the ob-

ject cannot possibly be over-wise and righteous, yet
as compared with the agent or subject, may be too
much.   No man can know, believe, or love God too
much, nor answerable to his perfections. But one
may possibly be transported with so earnest a desire
of God, Christ, Christian society, holiness and heaven, as may be more than head and health can bear;
and so it may be too much for the subject.   3. Therefore the probable effects must be weighed.   He that
should meditate, read, yea, love God so intensely as
to distract him, would do it overmuch.   He that
would do a good work precisely, when the exactness
would hinder the substance of another, perhaps a better, would be righteous overmuch.   And I thought
this the case sometimes of my dear wife; 1. She set
her head and heart so intensely upon doing good,
that her head and body would hardly bear it.   As holy, set meditation is no duty to a melancholy person
that cannot do it without confusion and danger of
distraction; so many other duties are no duties,
when they will do more harm than good.   2. And a
man is limited in his capacity and his time.   No man
can do all the good he would; and to omit a greater
for the better doing of a lesser, or to omit the substance of the one for exacter doing of another, I
thought was to be unrighteous by being righteous
overmuch.   She (and some others) thought I had
done better to have written fewer books, and to have
done those few better.   I thought, while I wrote
none needlessly, the modal imperfection of two was
less evil than the total omission of one.   She thought
I should have spent more time in religious exercise
with her, my family, and my neighbours, though I
had written less.   I thought there were many to do

such work, that would not do mine; and that I chose the greatest, which I durst not omit, and could not do both in the measure that I desired else to have done.

11. As she saith (before cited) herself, that *if she was but in a condition, in which God's service was costly to her, it would make her know whether she was sincere or not*; so she had her wish, and proved her sincerity by her costliest obedience. It cost her not only her labour and estate, but somewhat of her trouble of body and mind; for her knife was too keen, and cut the sheath. Her desires were more earnestly set on doing good, than her tender mind and head could well bear; for indeed her great infirmity was the four passions of love, desire, fear, and trouble of mind. Anger she either had very little, next none, or little made it known. She rarely ever spake in an angry manner, she could not well bear to hear one speak loud, or hastily, or eagerly, or angrily, even to those that deserved it. My temper in this she blamed, as too quick and earnest. When her servants did any fault unwillingly, she scarcely ever told them of it; when one lost ten pounds worth of linen in carriage carelessly, and another ten pounds worth of plate by negligence, she shewed no anger at any such thing. If servants had done amiss, and we could not prove it, or knew not which did it, she would never ask them herself, nor suffer others, lest it should tempt them to hide it by a lie (unless it were a servant that feared God, and would not lie).

I took her deep and long sense of the faults of over-loved and obliged persons, to be one of her greatest faults. But no one was ever readier to forgive a fault confessed, or which weakness and religious differ-

sect caused. I will give but one instance: The
good woman of whom she used to hire the rooms over
St. James's market-house, was greatly against the
Common Prayer, and first made my wife feel whether
I meant to use it, before she would take it. I told
her I intended not to use it, but would not promise
her. Upon that my wife told her that I would not.
After this I caused the reader to read the Psalms,
Chapters, Creed, Decalogue, and I used the Lord's-
prayer; and I openly told them, that we met not as
a separated, distinct church, but for the time to supply the notorious necessities of the people, and as
helpers of the allowed ministry. The good woman
thought this had been reading the Common-prayer,
and in a letter which I now find, accused my wife with
five or six vehement charges, for telling her I would
not read the Common-prayer. My wife was of my
mind for the matter; but greatly offended with me
for seeming to do it for the avoiding of danger; and
was so far from not pardoning these false, smart ac-
cusations, that she never once blamed the good woman, but loved her, tended her, and relieved her in
sickness to the death, but hardly forgave me; and
yet drew me from all other places, if the ministers
were not of my mind (by prudent diversity).

Much less did her sufferings from the times distemper her. She hath blamed me for naming in
print my losses, imprisonment, and other sufferings
by the bishops, as being over-selfish querulousness,
when I should rather with wonder be thankful for
the great mercy we yet enjoyed. Though I think I
never mentioned them as over-sensible of the sufferings, but as a necessary evincing of the nature of the
cause, and as part of the necessary history or matter

of fact in order to decide it. She as much disliked the silencing of the ministers, as any; but she did not love to hear it much complained of, save as the public loss; nor to hear Conformists talked against as a party; nor the faults of the conscientious sort of them aggravated in a siding, factious manner.

But (1.) She was prone to *overlove* her *relations*, and those good people, (poor as much as rich) whom she thought most upright. The love was good, but the degree was too passionate.

(2.) She *over-earnestly* desired their spiritual welfare. If these whom she overloved, had not been as good, and done as well as she would have them, in innocent behaviour, in piety, and (if rich) in liberality, it over-troubled her, and she could not bear it.

(3.) She was apt when she set her mind and heart upon some good work which she counted *great*, or the welfare of some dear friend, to be too much pleased in her expectations and self-made promises of the success; and then almost overturned with trouble when they disappointed her. And she too impatiently bore unkindnesses from the friends that were most dear to her, or whom she had much obliged. Her will was set upon good, but her weakness could not bear the crossing or frustration of it.

12. But the great infirmity which tyrannized over her, was a diseased *fearfulness*, against which she had little more freewill or power, than a man in an ague or frost, against shaking cold. Her nature was prone to it; and I said before, abundance of sad accidents made that, and trouble of mind, her malady. Besides (as she said) four times in danger of death. 2. And the storming of her mother's house by soldiers, firing part, killing, plundering, and threatening the

rest. 3. The awakenings of her conversion. 4. The
sentence of death by sickness presently, before her
peace was settled. 5. The fire next her lodgings in
Sweeting's-alley. 6. The burning of a merchant,
his wife and family, in *Lothbury*, over against her
brother *Upton*'s door. 7. The common terror and
confusion at *Dunstan*'s church in *Fleet-street*, when
they thought the church was falling on their heads
while I was preaching, and the people cast themselves down from the galleries. 8. Her mother's
death. 9. The friendless state she thought she was
then left in. 10. The great plague.* 11. The burning
of *London*.* 12. The crack and danger of her cham-
ber in *Aldersgate-street*. 13. The crack and confusion at *St. James*'s market-house. 14. The many
fires and talk of firing since. 15. The common rumours of murderings and massacres. 16. The death
and dangers of many of her friends, and my own illness. More than all these concurred to make *fear*
and *aptness to be troubled*, to be her disease; so that
she much dreamed of fire and murderers; and her
own dreams worked half as dangerously on her as re-
alities; so that she could not bear the clapping of a
door, or any thing that had suddenness, noise or

---

* The great Fire of London begun on the 2d of September,
1666, and in four days consumed nearly the whole of the city within
the walls. Great as this calamity was, yet it proved the providen-
tial cause of putting a stop to one of a far more tremendous nature.
The Plague, which for a series of ages had, with very short inter-
vals, visited our capital in its most dreadful forms, never appeared
there again after rebuilding the city in a more open and airy
manner. The last, the one referred to above, happened in the year
1665, when in about six months, at the lowest computation, a hundred and sixty thousand people fell by the destroying angel.

fierceness in it. But all this was more the malady
of her body than her soul; and I accounted had little
moral guilt: and I took it for an evidence of the
power of grace, that so timorous a person, 1. Had
overcome most of her fears of hell and God's deser-
tion. 2. And was more fearless of persecution, imprisonment, or losses and poverty thereby, than I, or
any that I remember to have known.

13. And though her spirits were so quick, and she
so apt to be troubled at men's sin whom she much
loved, she greatly differed from me in her bearing
with them, and carriage towards them. My temper
and judgment much led me to use my dependents,
servants and friends, according to the rules of church-
discipline; and if they heard not loving, private ad-
monitions once, twice, and thrice, to speak to them
more sharply, and then before others, and to turn
them off if yet they would not amend. But her way
was to oblige them by all the love, kindness and
bounty that she was able, and to bear with them year
after year while there was hope, and at last not to
desert them, but still use them so as she thought was
likeliest at least to keep them in a state of hope from
the badness which displicency might cause. I could
not have borne with a son, I think, as she could do,
where her kindness was at her own choice; and yet
she more disliked the least fault than I did, and was
more desirous of their greatest innocency and exactness.

14. Indeed she was so much for calmness, deliberation, and doing nothing rashly, and in haste, and
my condition and business, as well as temper, made
me do and speak much so suddenly, that she principally differed from me, and blamed me in this; every
considerable case and business she would have me

take time to think much of before I did it, or speak, or resolved of any thing. I knew the counsel was good for one that could stay, but not for one that must ride post : I thought still I had but a little time to live ; I thought some considerable work still called for haste. I have these forty years been sensible of the sin of losing time : I could not spare an hour : I thought I could understand the matters in question as well at a few thoughts as in many days ; and yet she (that had less work and more leisure, but) a far quicker apprehension than mine, was all for staying to consider, and against haste and eagerness in almost every thing ; and notwithstanding her over-quick and feeling temper, was all for mildness, calmness, gentleness, pleasingness and serenity.

15. She had an earnest desire of the conversion and salvation of her servants, and was greatly troubled that so many of them (though tolerable in their work) went away ignorant, or strange to true godliness, as they came ; and such as were truly converted with us she loved as children.

16. One infirmity made her faulty in the omission of much of her duty : she was wont to say, that she had from her childhood imprinted a deep fear and hatred of hypocrisy on her mind, that she could never do the outside of her duty, as to the speaking part, for fear of hypocrisy. I scarce ever met with a person that was abler to speak long, for matter and good language, without repetitions, even about religious things ; and few that had more desire that it were well done; and yet she could not do it herself for fear of seeming to be guilty of ostentation. In good company she would speak little of that which she most desired to hear. When I was at any time from

home, she would not pray in the family, though she could not endure to be without it. She would privately talk to the servants, and read good books to them. Most of the open speaking part of religion she omitted, through a diseased enmity to ostentation and hypocrisy. But of late years, when she saw me and others too sparing of profitable speech to young and ignorant people, she confessed that she saw her error, and that even an hypocrite, using but the words and outside of religion, was better to others than silence and unprofitable omission was.

17. Her household affairs she ordered with so great skill and decency, as that others much praised that which I was no fit judge of: I had been bred among plain, poor people, and I thought that so much washing of stairs and rooms, to keep them as clean as their trenchers and dishes, and so much ado about cleanliness and trifles, was a sinful curiosity, and expense of servants' time, who might that while have been reading some good book. But she that was otherwise bred, had somewhat other thoughts.

18. Her great tender impatiency lay much in her ears: she could not bear (without great reason) a disputing contradiction; nor yet to hear sad tidings, nor any hard prognostic; and it was because she felt the weakness of her own head, and for twenty years lived in too great fears of the overthrow of her understanding. And I was apt to think it was but a passionate, fanciful fear, and was too apt *to be impatient with her impatiency*, and with every *trouble* of her mind, not enough considering how great tenderness in all our discourse she needed; though I remember nothing else that ever I shewed impatience

to her in : but ever since her first danger, and strong
affection, I could hardly bear any signification of her
displeasure and discontent.   And she was wont oft
to say, ' It is a great mercy of God not to know what
will befal us in this world, nor how we shall be sick,
or suffer, or die, that our foreknowledge may not anticipate our sorrows, though in the general we should
always be ready.'

19. She was the greatest honourer of her mother,
and most sincerely loved her, that ever I knew a
child do to a parent.   She believed the promise of
the fifth commandment, and believed that it did im-
ply an answerable curse to them that broke it.   And
that as honouring parents hath even the promise of
blessings on earth, so the dishonouring them is like
to bring a curse upon the person or family that is
guilty of it : and that how great soever their present
prosperity may seem, it is coming and will overtake
them, either in their bodies, children, or estates.
The eye that mocketh at his father, and despiseth to
obey his mother; the ravens of the valley shall pick t
out, and the young eagles shall eat it; Prov. xxx. 17.
And such by *Moses's* law were to be put to death.
CURSED BE HE THAT SETTETH LIGHT BY
HIS FATHER OR HIS MOTHER; AND LET
ALL THE PEOPLE SAY, AMEN ; Deut. xxvii. 16.
And will God suspend it till the sinner saith, *Amen?*
O no.   And what is that person's case that liveth
under this curse of God ?   If the *body* escape it, and
posterity escape it, and the *estate* escape it, yea, and
a seared *conscience* escape it a few years, the *soul* will
not escape it for ever, without deep and thorough
repentance ; for Christ hath redeemed none but sin-

cere penitents from the curse. Yea, even such seldom escape the temporal, sharp chastisement.

And very worthy was her mother of her love and
honour; all her letters to her when she was from
home, I find now laid up by her as a treasure; I will
transcribe part of some of them, that you may perceive her plain and honest care of her children's souls.

20. In one, 1657, to this daughter at *Oxford*, she
writes thus :

"I cannot but put you in mind of your duty you
owe to God; I mean, that you see that you lose not
your time. If you be where you may improve your
time for grace, and getting down sin, I shall give
you my consent for your stay, (*with her brother Upton, Canon of Christ Church.*) But be sure you do
not deceive yourself herein, for God will not be
mocked. He that doth righteously and liveth to
Christ, shall enjoy all the blessings promised by God
to them that trust him, and obey him. I bless my
God, I have my health as well as I can wish; and
my heart runs out wholly to God, in seeking a blessing for children, and children's children. O that I
may prevail by prayer to see such hopes of you all,
upon good grounds, as will be a gracious return to
my prayers. This is my work. Be not you wanting
to yourself, your endeavours and prayers also are
necessary. Who knows but God will give you that
one thing necessary, which if you shall make it your
chiefest choice, shall never be taken from you? Let
the word of God dwell plentifully in you, that it may
be the rule of your life; which is the prayer of your
truly loving mother,

Mary, Hanmer."

21. In another, 1657, thus :

" I know not why you should write in tears, because of an apprehension of my displeasure; and
that you can see it at so great a distance, is strange
to me. If your information be of God, to whom you
appeal, look to it; if of men, believe it not. Many
false fears may arise, for want of the true fear of offending a good and gracious God: all your fears,
and all your joys must be founded in him, or else
your life here will be very uncomfortable. Had not
I my comforts from my God, and not only in the
creature, I had sunk long since, and often in despair.
Take my experience, or rather hear the word of God,
which says, *It is better to trust in God, than to put
confidence in riches: it is better to trust in God, than
to put confidence in men.* Be well acquainted with
the will of God, and be sure in all things to please
him, and then all other cares and fears will be of no
value to you. O let it be your daily study, and let
me in writing see some fruits of your labours, before
I go hence and be seen here no more. Be not wanting to your own comforts, and you cannot displease
God nor your mother, who longs more after your
eternal good, than I can now utter. My love to you
all, and prayers for you all. I continue,

Your most tenderly loving mother,

M. H."

22. In another to *Oxford,* 1657.

" All will work for good to them that love God; I
hope you are one of those. The Lord direct your
paths, that you may work out your salvation with

fear and trembling in your youth, and not let time
slip till age, which will come (or death before it) on
all flesh, and an account must be given of the precious
time which we now neglect. I have more to say,
but when I see you, it will be done with more ease.
The Lord keep you all, and make you faithful till
death, that you may receive the crown of glory;
which is the prayer of her that tendereth the good of
your soul,

M. H."

23. *In 1659.* In another she writes thus:

" My dear Child,

   " My greatest trouble is, that I can
have no better account of your health of body; yet
surely the cure of the soul is of far more worth:
therefore I faint not: else I could not subsist under
the heavy stroke which I have justly deserved. Who
knows, but my sins may be some cause of thy distress
of soul? However, let us return to the Lord, and he
will heal all our breaches, and will bind up all our
sores, and will give us a house not made with hands,
eternal in the heavens, where we shall never be
forced asunder, and all infirmities shall be left behind; and we shall take up all pleasure in the enjoyment of our heavenly Redeemer. In the mean
time, let us with courage and confidence press hard
toward the mark, for the prize of that high calling
which was set before us; *for the things which are seen
are temporal, but the things which are not seen are
eternal.* I can go no further, but cannot forget to be
Thy truly loving mother,
M. H."

This was written to her in her sickness, when, for better air, she lay at old *Mr. Richard Foley*'s house at *Stourbridge*.

24. I have transcribed these, to shew the mind and care of the good gentlewoman, and what cause I and my neighbours had of compassion to her in her sorrows, when she was separated from an only son, whose welfare she had prosecuted with so strong affection, and long labour and patience, and began to have much comfort in this daughter whom she had formerly least valued, and thought she must so suddenly leave her. Let those that think these too little matters to be told the world, remember, that *nearness, love and sorrow*, may be allowed to make things greater to me, than they seem to those that are not so concerned in them; *and that Mr. Fox in his Book of Martyrs, publisheth a great number of as mean letters as any of these, even some of women, and some written to the martyrs, as well as those written by them.* And while I say that, I will add, that though for nineteen years I was so seldom from her, that she had few letters of mine, yet those which she had I find now among her reserved papers : and that you may see what it was that I thought she most desired, and what she herself most valued, I will here add one of them, not venturing to trouble such with more, as are affected little with any matters but their own, which is the case of most. I recite this rather than others, partly also as an act of repentance for those failings of her just expectations, by the neglect of such helps as I should have given her, which I had here mentioned. For though she oft said, that before she married me she expected more sourness, and unsuitableness than she found; yet I am sure that

she found less zeal, and holiness, and strictness in all words, and looks, and duties, and less help for her soul than she expected : and her temper was to aggravate a fault much more in her nearest and dearest friends than in any others, and to be far more troubled at them. But this use she made of my too cold and careless converse, and of all my impatiency with her impatience, and of all my hasty words, that she that had long thought she had no grace, because she reached not higher than almost any reach on earth, and because she had many passions and infirmities, perceived by me and many other esteemed teachers, that we were all as bad as she ; and therefore grace doth stand with more faultiness than she had imagined, and that all our teaching much excelled the frame of our souls and lives, and was much more worthy to be followed; and therefore that God would also pardon such failings as her own.

" Though I have received none from you, but one from *Mr. H.* I will not be avenged on you by the like. I have nothing of news or business to communicate, but to tell you, that we are all here yet as well as you left us, excepting what your absence causeth. And yet I must confess, I find that it is easier to be oft speaking to God, when I have nobody else to speak to, than when there are other competitors, expectants, or interpolators. Just as I can easier now fill my paper to thee, with some speech of God, when I have nothing else to put into it, than I can when many other matters are craving every one a place. It is our shame that the love and glory of God doth not silence every other suitor, and even in the midst of crowds and business take us up, and

press every creature and occasion for their service.
But while we are weak, and compassed with flesh,
we must not only consider what we *should* do, but
what we *can* do. It is our great fault that we are no
skilfuller, and faithfuller in helping one another, that
we might miss each other on better reasons, than
merely from the inclinations of love. I hope God
will make us better hereafter, that when we are
asunder, each of us may say, ' I miss the help for
watchfulness and heavenliness, for true love and
thankfulness to God, which I was wont to have.'
But O, what an enemy is a naughty heart, which
maketh us unable for our duty alone, and makes us
need the help of others, and yet will not suffer us to
use it when we have it. When we are alone, it maketh us impediments to ourselves, and when we are
in company it maketh us impediments to others.
Yet is there none, no, not the weakest of Christians,
but there is much in them that we might improve.
But we are so bad and backward at it, that Satan too
commonly hath his end, in making us unprofitable
to each other. If a good horse, or a good house be
a valuable mercy, how much more is a good friend?
But art and industry are necessary to the improvement. And no wonder when we fetch not the help
and comfort which we might have from God, from
Christ himself, from heaven, from Scripture, for
want of improving skill and industry. O how easy
is it, when our friends are taken from us, to say,
' Thus and thus I might, and should have used them,'
rather than so to use them while we have them ! I
hope God will help me to make some better use of
thee while we are together : and at a distance, O let
not a hearty request to God for each other, be any

day wanting. Dear heart, the time of our mutual help is short (O let us use it accordingly); but the time of our reaping the fruit of this, and all holy endeavours, and preparatory mercies, will be endless. Yet a little while, and we shall be both with Christ. He is willing of us, and I hope we are willing of him, and of his grace, though the flesh be weak. I am absent, but God is still with you, your daily Guide and Keeper; and I hope you will labour to make him your daily comfort. And now you have none to divert and hinder you to say, *When I awake, I am still with thee.* And when you are up, *I have set the Lord always before me; because he is at my right hand, I shall not be moved.* And when thoughts crowd in, *In the multitude of my thoughts within me, thy comforts delight my soul.* And when thoughts would trouble and perplex you, *My meditation of him shall be sweet, and I will delight in the Lord.* And when your wants and duty call you to him, *It is good for me to draw nigh to God.*

"All other comforts will be, as the things are which we take comfort in; that is, helpful if the things be helpful, and used but as helps: hurtful if the things be hurtful, or hurtfully used; vain if the things be vain; short if the things be transitory; and durable if the things are durable to us. And this is the chief comfort which you and I must have in one another, that is, as helpful towards God, and as our converse with him will be durable. The Lord forgive my great unprofitableness, and the sin that brought me under any disabilities to answer your earnest and honest desires of greater helps than I afford you, and help me yet to amend it towards you. But though my soul be faulty and dull, and my strength of nature fail, be sure that he will be a thousandfold better to thee, even here, than such crooked, feeble, useless things, as is

Thy R. B."

From *Hampden.*

CHAP. IX.

Of her bodily Infirmities, and her Death.

1. HER diseased fearfulness, and many former sicknesses, I have mentioned before. A great pain of the head held her from her youth, two or three days every fortnight, or little more; and upon every thing that did irritate the matter, she had a constant straitness in the lungs, a great incapacity of much exercise, motion, or any heating thing. Ever since her sickness, 1659, she hath lived in an ill-conceited fear of distraction, which greatly hurt her; it was because she had an aunt long so, deceased, and her parents were naturally passionate, and her spirits over-quick, and her blood thin and mobile; and though wisdom hid it from others in her converse, she felt the trouble of her own mind in things, as aforesaid, that much displeased her; and so lived in a constant fear, which tended to have brought on her what she feared: but her understanding was so far from failing, that it was higher and clearer than other people's; but like the treble strings of a lute strained up to the highest, sweet, but in continual danger.

2. About three years ago, by the mis-persuasion of a friend, drinking against the cholic a spoonful of powdered ginger every morning, near a quarter of a

year together, and then falling into some overwhelm-
ing thoughts; besides it overthrew her head for a
few days, but God, in great mercy, soon restored her.

3. Ever since that time her head-ach abated, and
she complained of a pain in one of her breasts, and her
incurable timorousness settled her in a conceit that
she should have a cancer (which I saw no great cause
to fear); but she could neither endure to hear that it
was none, or that it was; but in fearing uncertainty,
prepared constantly for a sad death: and several
friends, neighbours and relations, lately dying of can-
cers, increased her fear; but she seemed to be prepared cheerfully to undergo it.

4. The many and weekly rumours of plots, firings,
massacres, &c. much increased this fear, as is aforesaid; and the death of very many neighbours, young,
strong, and excellent Christians, of greatest use, and
many near friends, did greatly add to her sadness and
expectations of death. But little of this was seen to
any; she purposely carried it pleasantly, and as mer-
rily to others, when she was troubled.

5. The fears of a cancer made her take the waters
for physic often, and she kept down her body so in
her diet, that about five ounces of milk, or milk and
water, with a little chocolate in it, morning and
night, and about one or two bits at dinner was her
diet for many years.

6. At last, about ten weeks before her sickness, almost all her pain went out of her breast, and all fixed
in a constant pain upon the right kidney, and
with the pain a stoppage took place which caused
her much inconvenience. She divers days drank
Barnet Waters; but I think they were the last
occasion of her sickness, and too much Tincture of

Amber, which worked too powerfully on her brain, and suddenly cast her into strong disturbance and de-liration; in which, though the physicians, with great kindness and care, did omit nothing in their power, she died the twelfth day. She fell sick on *Friday, June 3, 1681,* and died *June 14.*

7. Though her understanding never perfectly return-ed, she had a very strong remembrance of the affect-ing passages of her life, from her childhood. *Mrs. Corbet* (whom she dearly loved, and had newly got into the house to be her companion), with others, standing by, she cried out to me, *My mother is in hea-ven, and Mr. Corbet is in heaven, and thou and I shall be in heaven.* And even in her last weakness was persuaded of her salvation.

8. She oft shewed us, that her soul did work to-wards God, crying out (complaining of her head), *Lord, let me know what I have done, for which I under-go all this. Lord, I submit, God chooseth best for me.* She desired me to pray by her, and seemed quietly to join to the end; she heard divers psalms, and a chapter read, and repeated part, and sung part of a psalm herself. The last words that she spake were; *My God help me, Lord have mercy upon me.*

9. God had been so many years training her up under the expectations and preparations for death, as made the case of her soul less grievous to me as no way doubting of her salvation; and knowing that a distracting fever, or frenzy, or an inflamma-tion, or disturbance of the animal spirits, or brain, or an imposthume may befal the best as soon as the worst. I thank God that she was never under any melancholy, which tempted her to any of those dole-

ful evils, which many scores, I think, that have been
with me (of several ways of education) have been
sadly tempted to. She near nineteen years lived with
me cheerful, wise, and a very useful life, in constant
love, and peace, and concord, except our differing
opinions about trivial occurrences, or our disputing
or differing mode of talk.

10. She was buried on *June 17*, in *Christ Church*,
in the ruins, in her own mother's grave. The grave
was the highest, next the old altar or table in the
chancel, on which, this her daughter had caused a
very fair, rich, large marble stone to be laid, *Anno*
1661, about twenty years ago; on which I caused
to be written her titles, and some Latin verses, and
these English ones:

"Thus must thy flesh to silent dust descend,
Thy mirth and worldly pleasure thus will end :
Then happy, holy souls, but woe to those
Who heaven forgot, and earthly pleasures chose :
Hear now this preaching grave : without delay,
Believe, repent, and work while it is day."

But *Christ's Church* on earth is liable to those
changes of which the *Jerusalem* above is in no danger. In the doleful flames of *London*, 1666, the fall
of the church broke this great marble all to pieces,
and it proved no lasting monument; and I hope this
paper monument, erected by one that is following,
even at the door, in some passion indeed of love and
grief, but in sincerity of truth, will be more publicly
useful and durable than that marble stone was,

CHAP. X.

*Some Uses proposed to the Reader from this History,
as the Reasons why I wrote it.*

IF this narrative be useless to the readers, it must
needs be the sin of the publisher; for idle writing is
worse than idle words. But I think it useful (with
that which followeth) to all these ends to considering
men.

1. It may help to convince those that are inclined
to *Sadduceism*, or infidelity, and believe not the testimony of the sanctifying Spirit to the truth of the
Word of God, but take holiness, as it differs from
heathen morality, to be but fancy, hypocrisy, custom, or self-conceit. A man that never felt the
working of God's special grace on his own heart, is
hardly brought to believe that others have that which
he never had himself. And this turneth usually to
diabolical malignity, inclining them to hate those,
and revile or despise them as deluded, proud, fanatic
hypocrites, who pretend to be any better than they
are, or to have that which they take to be but a conceit. All their religious thoughts they take for the
dreams of crazed, or proud persons; and their holy
discourse and prayers, but for canting, or vain bab-
bling. But acquaintance, if intimate with gracious
persons, might convince them of their mortal error;
and true history methinks may do much towards it.

2. I confess, with thanks to God, that having these
forty years found that all our holiness and comfort
depends upon our certain persuasion of the life of
retribution following, and that our certainty of this

depends upon our certain belief of the Holy Scriptures; and we being here in the dark, and too apt
to doubt of all that we see not, there are several sensible, or experienced present certainties, which have
been a great succour to my faith, to save me from
temptations to unbelief and doubting, and confirm
my assurance that the Scripture is God's word.

I. In that I undoubtedly see and hear, that through
all the world there is just such a pravity in human
nature, as the Scripture describeth for original sin;
which cannot be the state of man's integrity, when
his reason is convinced of much of the duty to God,
man and himself, which he will not do, and of most
of the great sins which he will not forsake.

II. I see the Scripture clearly verified in mentioning the common enmity and war between the
serpent's and the holy seed; it is notorious through
the world, in all ages and countries, an enmity which
no relation or interest reconcileth.

III. I feel and see the Scripture verified, which
describeth all the temptations of Satan, and the secret war within us between the Spirit and the flesh.

IV. And I feel and see the Scripture fulfilled, which
promiseth a blessing on God's word, and his ordinances.

V. And I feel and see the Scripture fulfilled, which
describeth the renewing work of the Holy Ghost,
and the spiritual difference of the sanctified from all
others. This is not only in myself, but in others (O
how many hundred holy persons have I known) the
witness of Christ's truth and power; and as *Joshua's*
and *Caleb's* bunch of grapes, to assure me of the
land of promise, and God's truth which I see fulfilled

in them. Can I doubt of holiness when I feel it, and see it in the effects?

VI. Even as it persuadeth me the more easily to believe that there are devils, when I see their very nature and works, in devils incarnate, and see what a kingdom he plainly ruleth in the world; and to believe that there is a hell, when I see so much of hell on earth.

3. It may teach us that the state of godliness is not to be judged of by the fears and sorrows in which it usually begins: a man's life is not like his infancy at his birth. The fears and penitent sorrows which foolish, fleshly sinners fly from, do tend to everlasting peace and joy: and perfect love will cast out all tormenting fears, unless it be those of a timorous diseased temper, which have more of sickness than of sin, and will be laid aside with the body, which was their cause. A life of peace and joy on earth *may succeed* the tremblings of the new-born convert; but a life of full everlasting joy will certainly succeed the perseverance and victory of every believing holy soul.

4. It may warn all to take heed of expecting too much from so frail and bad a thing as man. My dear wife did look for more good in me, and more help from me than she found, especially lately in my weakness and decay. We are all like pictures that must not be looked on too near. They that come near us find more faults and badness in us than others at a distance know.

5. It should greatly warn us to take heed of small beginnings; even a spark of affection, honest in the kind, may kindle a flame not easily quenched. How great a matter may a little fire kindle! Almost all

sin beginneth in a seed or spark, which is very hardly known to be a sin or danger.

6. Yea, it should warn all to keep all the *thoughts*, *affections* and *passions* under a constant watch and obedience to God; and know first, whether God command them and allow them.

7. And this history may teach us, that though God usually begin (as is said) our conversion in *fear* and *penitent sorrows*, it is holy and heavenly joy which it tendeth to, as more desirable; and we should chiefly seek, and should labour to moderate fear and sorrow, and not think we can never have enough. It is too common an error with honest souls, to think that a hard heart lieth most in want of sorrow and tears, when as it lieth most in want of a tractable compliance, and yielding to the commands and will of God, and in an iron neck, and obstinate disobedience to God; and to think that a new and tender heart is principally a heart that can weep and mourn, when it is chiefly a heart that easily receiveth all the impressions of God's commands, and promises, and threats, and easily yieldeth to his known will.

8. And this may greatly warn us to fear and avoid *selfwilledness*; I mean, a will of our own that runs before the will of God, and is too much set on any thing which God hath not promised, and knows not how to bear a frustration or denial, but saith as *Rachel, Give it me, or I die.* We must learn to follow, and not to lead, and to say, 'The will of the Lord be done; not mine, Lord, but thine;' and in every estate to be content. There is no *rest* but in *God's will*.

9. Yet this tells us, that God dealeth better with his weak servants than they deserve, and turneth

that ofttimes to their good, which they deserved should have been their greatest suffering.

10. This history (and my great experience) saith, that *there is a friend that sticketh closer than a brother;* Prov. xviii. 24.; and that it was God's Spirit that said, *Thy own friend, and thy father's friend forsake not: neither go into thy brother's house in the day of thy calamity; for better is a neighbour that is near, than a brother that is far off;* Prov. xxvii. 10.

11. This history tells us how great a mercy it is to have a body meet to serve the soul, and how great an affliction to have an unruly inclination from the body's temper; and what a tyrant excessive fear is, and how great a blessing it is to have such a passion as faith can rule, and easily quiet.

12. It tells you also how manifold temptations and afflictions God's servants are liable to in this life.

13. And it tells you, that our greatest good or evil is nearest us. Next God, the best is in our souls; and there is the worst; and next in our bodies, and next in our nearest friends. And it may teach all to expect their greatest sorrows from those, or that which they most excessively love, and from whom they have the highest expectations: only God cannot be loved more than he deserveth. Sorrow beginneth in *inordinate love,* and joy in *good.*

14. And it tells us, that God's service lieth more in deeds than in words. My dear wife was faulty indeed in talking so little of religion in company (except it were irresistibly to confute in a few words an opposer, or reviler of religion). But her religion lay in *doing* more than talk.

15. Yet her example tells us, that it is one of Sa-

tan's wiles to draw us to one sin to avoid another;
and to make us think that nothing is a due that hath
great inconveniences, or which we can foresee some
men will receive hurt from; and so to be unrighteous
by being righteous overmuch, and leave much un-
done for fear of doing it amiss; by which rule we
should scarce ever do any thing that God commands;
He that observeth the winds shall not sow, and he that
regardeth the clouds shall not reap; Eccles. xi. 4. I
speak this on her (at last confessed) error of omitting
seasonable speech and duty to avoid hypocrisy and
ostentation, which my great friend, Judge *Hale,* was
just so guilty of, as I know, and the writers of his
life confess; he would make no great show of zeal
in religion, lest if he did any thing amiss, religion
should be reproached for his sake. Cardinal *Rich-*
lieu was wont to say (as is written of him), that he
hated no counsellers more than those that were always
saying, *Let us do it better;* by that hindering the doing of much at all.

16. You see here that suitableness in religious
judgment and disposition preserveth faster love and
concord (as it did with us) than suitableness in age,
education and wealth; but yet those should not be
imprudently neglected. Nothing causeth so near,
and fast, and comfortable a union, as to be united in
one God, one Christ, one Spirit, one faith, one church,
one hope of heavenly glory; yet accidental unsuitableness should be avoided as far as may be.

17. There are some great men who know their
own names, who (as I have most credible information) have, to greater than themselves, represented
me not only as covetous, but as mutable for my marriage.

To whom I now give this satisfaction. 1. As to covetousness, my vindication is a matter unfit for the ears of the world, if reverend men's backbitings (the same that troubles our common peace) did not make it partly necessary. Through God's mercy, and her prudent care, I lived in plenty, and so do still, though not without being greatly beholden to divers friends; and I am not poorer than when I married; but it is not by marriage, nor by any thing that was her's before.

2. And as to my mutability. Whereas one of them reports that I said to him, *that I thought the marriage of ministers had so great inconveniences, that though necessity made it lawful, yet it was but lawful; that is, to be avoided as far as lawfully we may.* I answer, that I did say so to him; and I never changed my judgment; yea, my wife lived and died in the same mind. And I here freely advise all ministers that have not some kind of necessity, to think of these few reasons among many.

1. The work of the sacred ministry is enough to take up the whole man, if he had the strength and parts of many men. O how much is there to do oftentimes with one ignorant, or scandalous, or sad, despairing soul! And who is sufficient for all that is to be done to hundreds or thousands? In the primitive church every congregation had many ministers; but covetousness of clergy and people will now scarce allow two to very great parishes. I did not marry till I was silenced and ejected, and had no flock or pastoral cure. Believe it, he that will have a wife, must spend much of his time in conference, prayer, and other family-duties with her. And if he have children, O how much care, time, and labour will

they require! I know it, though I have none. And he that hath servants, must spend time in teaching them, and in other duties for them; besides the time, and perhaps caring thoughts that all his family expenses and affairs will require. And then it will disquiet a man's mind to think that he must neglect his family or his flock, and hath undertaken more than he can do. My conscience hath forced me many times to omit secret prayer with my wife when she desired it, for want of time, not daring to omit far greater work.

2. And a minister can scarce look to win much on his flock, if he be not able to oblige them by gifts of charity and liberality. And a married man hath seldom any thing to spare, especially if he have children that must be provided for, all will seem too little for them. Or if he have none, housekeeping is chargeable, when a single man may have entertainment at easy rates; and most women are weak, and apt to live in fear of want, if not in covetousness, and have many wants, real or fancied, of their own to be supplied.

3. In a word, St Paul's own words are plain to others, but concern ministers much more than other men; *I would that all men were as I myself—It is good for them if they abide even as I;* 1 Cor. vii. 7, 8. *Such shall have trouble in the flesh;* ver. 28. *I would have you without carefulness. He that is unmarried, careth for the things that belong to the Lord, how he may please the Lord: but he that is married, careth for the things of the world, how he may please his wife;* ver. 32. This is true. And believe it, both caring for the things of the world, and caring to please one another, are businesses, and troublesome businesses;

care for house-rent, for children, for servant's wages, for food and raiment, but above all for debts, are very troublesome things; and if cares choke the word in hearers, they will be very unfit for the mind of a student, and a man that should still dwell on holy things.

And the pleasing of a wife is usually no easy task: there is an unsuitableness in the best, and wisest, and likest. Faces are not so unlike as the apprehensions of the mind. They that agree in religion, in love and interest, yet may have daily different apprehensions about occasional occurrences, persons, things, words, &c. That will seem the best way to one that seems worst to the other. And passions are apt to succeed, and serve these differences. Very good people are very hard to be pleased: my own dear wife had high desires of my doing, and speaking better than I did, but my badness made it hard to me to do better. But this was my benefit; for it was but to put me on to be better: as God himself will be pleased: that it is hard to please God and holy persons, is only our fault. But there are too many that will not be pleased, unless you will contribute to their sin, their pride; their wastefulness, their superfluities and childish fancies, their covetousness and passions: and too many who have such passion, that it requireth greater skill to please them, than almost any, the wisest can attain. And the discontents and displeasure of one that is so near you, will be as thorns or nettles in your bed.

And *Paul* concludeth, to be unmarried is the *better,* that we may *attend the Lord without distraction;* ver. 35. 38.

And what need we more than Christ's own words,—

Matt. xix. 10—12.? When they said then, *It is not good to marry*, he answers, *All men cannot receive this saying, save they to whom it is given; for there are some eunuchs, who were so born from their mother's womb; and there are some eunuchs who were made eunuchs by men; and there be eunuchs which have made themselves eunuchs for the kingdom of heaven's sake: he that is able to receive it, let him receive it.*

O how many sad and careful hours might many a minister have prevented; and how much more good might he have done, if (being under no necessity) he had been sooner wise in this!

18. Another use of this history is, to shew men; that it is not God's or our enemies' afflicting us in worldly losses or sufferings (especially when we suffer for righteousness' sake) which is half so painful, as our own inward infirmities. A man's spirit can bear his infirmities of outward crosses; but a wounded spirit who can bear! My poor wife made nothing of prisons, distrainings, reproaches, and such crosses; but her burden was most inward, from her own tenderness, and next from those whom she overloved. And for mine own part, all that ever either enemies or friends have done against me, is but a trifle to me, in comparison of the daily burden of a pained body, and the weakness of my soul in faith, hope, love, and heavenly desires and delights.

19. And here you may see, how necessary patience is, and to have a mind fortified beforehand against all sorts of sufferings, that in our patience we may possess our souls. And that the dearest friends must expect to find much in one another that must be borne with, and exercise our patience: we are all imperfect. It hath made me many a time

wonder at the prelates, that can think it the way to
the concord of millions, to force them to consent to
all their impositions, even of words, and promises,
and ceremonies, and that in things where conscience
must be most cautelous; whereas even husband and
wife, master and servants have almost daily differences in judging of their common affairs.

20. And by this history you may see, how little
cause we have to be over-serious about any worldly
matters, and to mind and do them with too much
intenseness of affection; and how necessary it is to
possess them as if we possessed them not, seeing the
time is short, and the fashion of this world passeth
away. And how reasonable it is, that if we love
God, ourselves, yea, or our friends, that we should
long to be with Christ, where they are far more
amiable than here, and where in the city of God, the
Jerusalem above, we shall delightfully dwell with
them for ever: whereas here we were still sure to
stay with them but a little while. And had we here
known Christ after the flesh, we should so know him
no more: whereas *believing* that we shall soon be
with him, even those that never saw him, may rejoice with joy unspeakable and full of glory.

21. Lastly, here you may see that as God's servants have not their portion of good things in this
life, so they may have the same sicknesses and manner of death as others: *Lazarus* may lie and die in
his sores, among the dogs at the door, when *Dives*
may have a pompous life and funeral. There is no
judging of a man's sincerity, or of his future state,
by his disease, or by his diseased deathbed words.
He that liveth to God, shall die safely into the hand
of God, though a fever or deliration hinder him from

knowing this, till experience and sudden possession of heaven convince him. *Blessed are the dead that die in the Lord, from henceforth; yea, saith the Spirit, that they may rest from their labours, and their works do follow them;* Rev. xiv. 13. Therefore in our greatest straits and sufferings, let us comfort one another with these words, *That we shall for ever be with the Lord.* Had I been to possess the company of my friends in this life only, how short would our comfortable converse have been! But now I shall live with them in the heavenly city of God for ever. And they being there of the same mind with my forgiving God and Saviour, will forgive all my failings, neglects and injuries, as God forgiveth them and me. The Lord gave, and the Lord hath taken away; and he hath taken away but that upon my desert, which he had given me undeservedly near nineteen years. Blessed be the name of the Lord. I am waiting to be next: the door is open. Death will quickly draw the veil, and make us see how near we were to God and one another, and did not (sufficiently) know it. Farewell vain world, and welcome true everlasting life.

Hoc migraturus scripsi sub imagine Carmen.

FAREWELL vain world: As thou hast been to me
Dust and a shadow, such I leave to thee.
The unseen *life* and *substance* I commit
To him that's *Substance, Life, Light, Love to it.*
Some *leaves* and *fruit* are dropt for soil and seed;
Heaven's heirs to generate; to heal and feed:
Them also thou wilt flatter and molest,
But shalt not keep from Everlasting Rest.

SOME ACCOUNT

OF

Mrs. MARY HANMER,

MOTHER OF MRS. BAXTER.

Taken principally from a Funeral Sermon preached at St. Mary Magdalene's Church, Milk Street, London, by Mr. Richard Baxter.

THE person whose death did occasion this account, was the widow first, of *Francis Charlton, Esq.,* and after of *Thomas Hanmer, Esq.* About five years ago (in 1656) she removed from her ancient habitation, at *Appley* in *Shropshire,* to *Kidderminster,* where she lived under my pastoral care till I was come up to *London:* and before she had lived there a twelvemonth (for thither she removed), she died of the fever, then very common in the city.

She lived among us an example of prudence, gravity, sobriety, righteousness, piety, charity and self-denial, and was truly what I have described her to be, and much more ; for I use not to flatter the living, much less the dead. And though I had personal acquaintance with her for no longer a time than I have mentioned, yet I think it worthy the mentioning, which I understand by comparing her last years with what is said of her former time, by those that were then nearest to her, and so were at her death, that whereas as I have said, sudden passion was the sin that she was wont much to complain of, she had not con-

tented herself with mere complainings, but so effectually resisted them, and applied God's remedies for
the healing of her nature, that the success was very
much observed by those about her, and the change
and cure so great herein, as was a comfort to her
nearest relations, that had the benefit of her converse : which I mention as a thing that shews us, 1.
That even the infirmities that are founded in nature
and temperature of body, are curable so far as they
fall under the dominion of a sanctified will. 2. That
even in age, when such passions usually get ground,
and infirmities of mind increase with infirmities of
body, yet grace can effectually do its work. 3. That
to attend God in his means, for the subduing of any
corruption, is not in vain.   4. That as God hath promised growth of grace, and flourishing in old age,
so in his way we may expect the fulfilling of his promise. 5. That as grace increaseth, infirmities and
corruptions of the soul will vanish.

This makes me call to mind that she was once so
much taken with a sermon which I preached, at the
funeral of a holy, aged woman,* and so sensibly oft
recited the text itself as much affecting her ; (*For
which cause we faint not ; but though our outward man
perish, yet the inward man is renewed day by day, &c.;
2 Cor. iv. 16, 17 ;) that I am persuaded both the

_____

* Good old Mrs. Doughty, sometime of Shrewsbury, who had
long walked with God, and longed to be with him ; and was
among us an excellent example of holiness, blamelessness, contempt
of the world, constancy, patience, humility, and (which makes it
strange) a great and constant desire to die, though she was still
complaining of doubtings and weakness of assurance.

text itself, and the example opened (and well known) to her, did her much good.

What cause have we now to mix our sorrows for our deceased friend, with the joys of faith for her felicity! We have left the body to the earth, and that is our lawful sorrow, for it is the fruit of sin. But her spirit is received by Jesus Christ; and that must be our joy, if we will behave ourselves as true believers. If we can suffer with her, should we not rejoice also with her? And if the joy be far greater to the soul with Christ, than the ruined state of the body can be lamentable, it is but reason that our joy should be greater for her joy, than our sorrow for the dissolution of the flesh. We that should not much lament the passage of a friend beyond the seas, if it were to be advanced to a kingdom, should less lament the passage of a soul to Christ, if it were not for the remnant of our woeful unbelief.

She is arrived at the everlasting rest, where the burden of corruption, the contradictions of the flesh, the molestations of the tempter, the troubles of the world, and the injuries of malicious men, are all kept out, and shall never more disturb her peace. She hath left us in these storms, who have more cause to weep for ourselves and for our children that have yet so much to do and suffer, and so many dangers to pass through, than for the souls that are at rest with Christ. We are capable of no higher hopes than to attain that state of blessedness which her soul possesseth. And shall we make that the matter of our lamentation as to her, which we make the matter of our hopes as to ourselves? Do we labour earnestly to come thither, and yet lament that she is

there? You will say, It is not because she is cloth-
ed upon with the house from heaven, but that she is
unclothed of the flesh: But is there any other passage than death unto immortality? Must we not be
unclothed, before the garments of glory can be put
on? She bemoaneth not her own dissolved body:
the glorified soul can easily bear the corruption of
the flesh: and if you saw but what the soul enjoyeth,
you would be like-minded, and be moderate in your
grief. Love not yourselves so as to be unjust and
unmerciful in your desires to your friends. Let Satan
desire to keep them out of heaven, but do not you
desire it. You may desire your own good, but not
so as to deprive your friends of theirs; yea, of a
greater good, that you may have a lesser by it. And
if it be their company that you desire, in reason you
should be glad that they are gone to dwell where you
must dwell for ever, and therefore may for ever have
their company. Had they staid on earth, you would
have had their company but a little while, because
you must make so short a stay yourselves. Let them
therefore begin their journey before you, and grudge
not that they are first at home, as long as you expect
to find them there. In the meantime, he that called
them from you, hath not left you comfortless: he is
with you himself, who is better than a mother, or
than ten thousand friends. When grief or negligence
hindereth you from observing him, yet he is with you,
and holdeth you up, and tenderly provideth for you.
Though turbulent passions injuriously question all
his love, and cause you to give him unmannerly and
unthankful words, yet still he beareth with you, and
forgiveth all, and doth not forsake you for your
peevishness and weakness, because you are his chil-

dren, and he knoweth that you mean not to forsake him. Rebuke your passions, and calm your minds; reclaim your thoughts, and cast away the bitterness of suspicious, quarrelsome unbelief; and then you may perceive the presence of your dearest friend and Lord; who is enough for you, though you had no other friend. Without him all the friends on earth would be but silly comforters, and leave you as at the gates of hell: without him all the angels and saints in heaven would never make it a heaven to you. Grieve not too much that one of your candles is put out, while you have the sun: or if indeed it be not day with any of you, or the sun be clouded or eclipsed, let that rather be the matter of your grief: find out the cause, and presently submit, and seek reconciliation. Or if you are deprived of this light, because you are yet asleep in sin, hearken to his call, and rub your eyes. *Awake thou that sleepest, and arise from the dead, and Christ shall give thee light;* Eph. v. 14. *Knowing that it is now high time to awake out of sleep; our salvation being nearer than when we first believed: the night is far spent, the day of eternal light is even at hand: cast off therefore the works of darkness, and put on all the armour of light: walk honestly and decently as in the day;* Rom. xiii. 11—14. And whatever you do, make sure of the friend that never dieth, and never shall be separated from you, and when you die, will certainly receive the souls which you commend unto him.

And here, though contrary to my custom, I shall make some more particular mention of our deceased friend, on several accounts. 1. In prosecution of this use that now we are upon, that you may see in the evidences of her happiness, how little cause you have to indulge extraordinary grief on her account, and how much cause to moderate your sense of our loss with the sense of her felicity.   2. That you may have the benefit of her example for your imitation, especially her children that are bound to observe the holy *actions* as well as *instructions* of a mother.   3. For the honour of Christ, and his grace, and his servant.   For as God hath promised to honour those that honour him, (1 Sam. ii. 30,) and Christ hath said, *If any man serve me, him will my Father honour,* (John xii. 26,) so I know Christ will not take it ill to be honoured in his members, and to have his ministers subserve him in so excellent a work.   It is a very considerable part of the love or hatred, honour or dishonour that Christ hath in the world, which he receiveth as he appeareth in his followers.   He that will not see a cup of cold water given to one of them go unrewarded, and will tell those at the last day that did or did not visit or relieve them, that they did or did it not to him, will now expect it from me as my duty, to give him the honour of his grace in his deceased servant, and I doubt not will accordingly accept it, when it is no other indeed than his own honour that is my end, and nothing but the words of truth and soberness shall be the means.

And here I shall make so great a transition as shall retain my account in the narrow compass of the time in which she lived near me and under my care, and in my familiar acquaintance, omitting all the rest of her life, that none may say I speak but by hearsay of things which I am uncertain of; and I will confine it also to those special gifts and graces in which she was eminent, that I may not take you up with a description of a Christian as such, and tell

you only of that good which she held but in common
with all other Christians. And if any thing that I
shall say were unknown to any reader that knew her,
let them know that it is because they knew her but
distantly, imperfectly, or by reports; and that my
advantage of near acquaintance did give me a just
assurance of what I say.

The graces which I discerned to be eminent in her,
were these: 1. She was eminent in her contempt of
the pride, and pomp, and pleasure, and vanity of the
world, and in her great averseness from all these. She
had an honest impatiency of the life which is common
among the rich and vain-glorious in the world. Vo-
luptuousness and sensuality, excess of drinking,
cards and dice she could not endure, whatever names
of good housekeeping or seemly deportment they
borrowed for a mask. In her apparel she went below the garb of others of her rank; indeed in such
plainness as did not notify her degree, but yet in such
a grave and decent habit, as notified her sobriety and
humility. She was a stranger to pastimes, and no
companion for time-wasters, as knowing, that persons so near eternity, that have so short a life and so
great a work, have no time to spare. Accordingly
in her latter days, she did (as those that grow wise
by experience of the vanity of the world) retire from
it, and cast it off before it cast off her. She betook
herself to the society of a people that were low in
the world, of humble, serious, upright lives, though
such as had been wholly strangers to her: and among
these poor inferior strangers she lived in contentment and quietness; desiring rather to converse with
those that would help her to redeem the time, in

prayer and edifying conference, than with those that would grieve her by consuming it on their lusts.

2. She was very prudent in her converse and affairs (allowing for the passion of her sex and age); and so escaped much of the inconveniences that else in so great and manifold businesses would have overwhelmed her. As a good man will guide his affairs with discretion, (Psal. cxii. 5,) so discretion will preserve him, and understanding will keep him, to deliver him from the way of the evil man, who leaveth the paths of uprightness to walk in the way of darkness; Prov. ii. 11—13.

3. She was seriously religious, without partiality, or any taint of siding or faction, or holding the faith of our Lord Jesus Christ in respect of persons. I never heard her speak against men or for men, as they differed in some small and tolerable things. She impartially heard any minister that was able, and godly, and sound in the main, and could bear with the weaknesses of ministers when they were faithful. Instead of owning the names or opinions of Prelatical, Presbyterian, Independent, or such like, she took up with the name and profession of a *Christian*, and loved a Christian as a Christian, without much respect to such different, tolerable opinions. Instead of troubling herself with needless scruples, and making up a religion of opinions and singularities, she studied faith and godliness, and lived upon the common certain truths, and well-known duties, which have been the old and beaten way, by which the universal church of Christ hath gone to heaven in former ages.

4. She was very impartial in her judgment about

particular cases; being the same in judging of the case of a child and a stranger; and no interest of children or other relations, could make her swerve from an equal judgment.

5. She very much preferred the spiritual welfare of her children before their temporal; looking on the former as the true felicity, and on the latter without it, but as a pleasant, voluntary misery.

6. Since I was acquainted with her, I always found her very ready to good works, according to her power.   And when she hath seen a poor man come to me, that she conjectured solicited me for relief, she hath reprehended me for keeping the case to myself, and not inviting her to contribute.   And I could never discern that she thought any thing so well bestowed, as that which relieved the necessities of the poor that were honest and industrious.

7. She had the wonderful mercy of a manlike, Christian, patient spirit, under all afflictions that did befal her, and under the multitude of troublesome businesses, that would have even distracted an impatient mind.   Though sudden anger was the sin that she much confessed herself; and therefore thought she wanted patience, yet I have oft wondered to see her bear up with the same alacrity and quietness, when *Job*'s messengers have brought her the tidings that would have overwhelmed an impatient soul. When law-suits and the great afflictions of her children have assaulted her like successive waves, which I feared would have borne her into the deep, if not devoured all her peace, she sustained all, as if no considerable change had been made against her, having the same God, and the same Christ, and pro-

G

mises, and hope, from which she fetched such real comfort and support, as shewed a real, serious faith.

8. She was always apt to put a good interpretation upon God's providences; like a right believer, that having the spirit of adoption, perceiveth fatherly love in all. She would not easily be persuaded that God meant her any harm; she was not apt to hearken to the enemy that accuseth God and his ways to man, as he accuseth man and his actions to God. She was none of those that are suspicious of God, and are still concluding death and ruin from all that he doth to them, and are gathering wrath from misinterpreted expressions of his love; who weep because of the smoke, before they can be warmed by the fire. *Yet God is good to Israel, and it shall go well with them that fear before him,* (Psal. lxxiii. 1. Eccles. viii. 13,) were her conclusions from the sharpest providences. She expected the morning in the darkest night; and judged not of the end by the beginning; but was always confident, if she could but entitle God in the case, that the issue would be good. She was not a murmurer against God, nor one that contended with her Maker; nor one that created calamity to herself by a self-troubling, unquiet mind. She patiently bore what God laid upon her, and made it not heavier by the additions of uncomfortable prognostics, and misgiving or repining thoughts. She had a great confidence in God, that he was doing good to her and her's in all; and where at present she saw any matter of grief, she much supported her soul with a belief that God would remove and overcome it in due time.

9. She was not troubled (that ever I discerned) with doubtings about her interest in Christ, and

about her own justification and salvation : but whether she reached to assurance or not, she had confident apprehensions of the love of God, and quietly reposed her soul upon his grace. Yet not secure through presumption or self-esteem, but comforting herself in the Lord her God : By this means she spent those hours in a cheerful performance of her duty, which many spend in fruitless self-vexation for the failings of their duty, or in mere inquiries whether they have grace or not ; and others spend in wrangling, perplexed controversies, about the manner or circumstances of duty. And I believe that she had more comfort from God by way of reward upon her sincere obedience, while she referred her soul to him, and rested on him, than many have that more anxiously perplex themselves about the discerning of their holiness, when they should be studying to be more holy, that it might discover itself. And by this means she was fit for praises and thanksgiving, and spent not her life in lamentations and complaints, and made not religion seem terrible to the ignorant, that judge of it by the faces and carriage of professors. She did not represent it to the world, as a morose and melancholy temper, but as the rational creature's cheerful obedience to his Maker, actuated by the sense of the wonderful love that is manifested in the Redeemer, and by the hopes of the purchased and promised felicity in the blessed sight and fruition of God. And I conjectured that her forementioned disposition to think well of God and of his providences, together with her long and manifold experience, (the great advantage of ancient, tried Christians,) did much conduce to free her from doubtings and disquieting fears, about her own sincerity and salvation. And I confess, if her life had not been answerable to her peace and confidence, I should not have thought the better, but the worse of her condition; nothing being more lamentable than to make haste to hell, through a wilful confidence that the danger is past, and that they are in the way to heaven as well as the most sanctified.

10. Lastly, I esteemed it the height of her attainment, that she never discovered any inordinate fears of death; but a cheerful readiness, willingness and desire, to be dissolved and be with Christ. This was her constant temper both in health and sickness, as far as I was able to observe. She would be frequently expressing how little reason she had to be desirous of longer life, and how much reason to be willing to depart. Divers times in dangerous sicknesses I have been with her, and never discerned any considerable averseness, dejectedness or fear. Many a time I have thought how great a mercy I should esteem it, if I had attained that measure of fearless willingness to lay down this flesh, as she had attained. Many a one that can make light of wants, or threats, or scorns, or any ordinary troubles, cannot submit so quietly and willingly to death. Many a one that can go through the labours of religion, and contemn opposition, and easily give all they have to the poor, and bear imprisonments, banishment or contempt, can never overcome the fear of death: so far even the father of lies spoke truth; *Skin for skin; yea, all that a man hath, will he give for his life;* Job ii. 4. I took it therefore for a high attainment, and extraordinary mercy to our deceased friend, that the king of terrors was not terrible to her. Though I doubt not but somewhat of averseness and fear is so radi-

cated in nature's self-preserving principle, as that it
is almost inseparable, yet in her I never discerned
any troublesome appearances of it. When I first
came to her in the beginning of her last sickness,
she suddenly passed the sentence of death upon herself, without any show of fear or trouble, when to us
the disease appeared not to be great: but when the
disease increased, her pains were so little, and the effect of the fever was so much in her head, that after
this she seemed not to esteem it mortal, being not
sensible of her case and danger. And so as she lived
without the fears of death, she seemed to us to die
without them: God by the nature of her disease removing death as out of her sight, when she came to
that weakness, in which else the encounter was like
to have been sharper than ever it was before. And
thus in one of the weaker sex, God hath showed us
that it is possible to live in holy confidence, and
peace, and quietness of mind, without distressing
griefs or fears, even in the midst of a troublesome
world, and of vexatious businesses, and with the afflictions of her dearest relations almost continually
before her: and that our quiet or disquiet, our peace
or trouble, dependeth more upon our inward strength
and temper, than upon our outward state, occasions,
or provocations: and that it is more in our hands,
than of any or all our friends or enemies, whether
we shall have a comfortable or uncomfortable life.

Her work is done: her enemies are conquered;
(except the remaining fruits of death upon a corrupting body, which the resurrection must conquer.)
Her danger, and temptations, and troubles, and fears
are at an end. She shall no more be discomfited
with evil tidings; nor any more partake with a mili-

tant church in the sorrows of her diseases or dis-
tresses. We are left within the reach of Satan's
assaults and malice; and of the rage and violence
which pride, and faction, and *Cainish* envy, and enmity to serious holiness, do ordinarily raise against
Christ's followers in the world. We are left among
the lying tongues of slanderous, malicious men; and
dwell in a wilderness among scorpions; where the
*sons of Belial, like Nabal, are such that a man cannot
speak to them;* 1 Sam. xxv. 17. *The best of them is
a briar, the most upright sharper than a thorn hedge;*
Mic. vii. 4. *(But the sons of Belial shall be all of
them as thorns thrust away, because they cannot be taken with hands, but the man that shall touch them must
be fenced with iron, and the staff of a spear, and they
shall be utterly burnt with fire in the place;* 2 Sam.
xxiii. 6, 7.) We are left among our weak, distempered, sinful, afflicted, lamenting friends; the sight
of whose calamities, and participation of their sufferings, maketh us feel the strokes that fall upon so
great a number, that we are never like to be free
from pain. But she is entered into the land of peace,
where pride and faction are shut out; where serpen-
tine enmity, malice and fury never come; where
there is no *Cain* to envy and destroy us; no *Sodom-
ites* to rage against us, and in their blindness to assault our doors; no *Ahithophels* to plot our ruin; no
Judas to betray us; no false-witnesses to accuse us;
no *Tertullus* to paint us out as pestilent fellows and
movers of sedition among the people; no *Rehum,
Shimshai,* or their society, to persuade the rulers that
the servants of the God of heaven are hurtful unto
kings, and against their interest and honour; (Ezra
iv. 9. 12—14. 22; v. 11.) no rabble to cry, Away

with them, it is not fit that they should live; no
Demas that will forsake us for the love of present
things; no such contentious, censorious friends as
Job's to afflict us, by adding to our affliction; no
cursed *Ham* to dishonour parents; no ambitious,
rebellious *Absalom* to molest us, or to lament; no
sinful, scandalous friends to be our grief; and which
is more than all, no earthly, sinful inclinations in
ourselves; no passions or infirmities; no languish-
ings of soul, no deadness, dulness, hard-heartedness,
or weaknesses of grace, no backwardness to God, or
estrangedness from him, nor fears or doubtings of
his love, nor frowns of his displeasure; none of these
do enter into that serene and holy region, nor ever
interrupt the joy of saints.

The great work is yet upon our hands, to fight out
the good fight, to finish our course, to run with patience the remainder of the race that is before us;
and as we must look to Jesus, the Author and Finisher of our faith, as our great exemplar, so must we
look to his saints and martyrs as our encouraging
examples under him. Put the case you were now
dying, (and O how near is it, and how sure!) what
would you need most if the day were come? That
is it that you need most now; look after it speedily
while you have time! Look after it seriously, if you
have the hearts of men, and sin have not turned you
into idiots or blocks. What a disgrace is it to mankind, to hear men commonly at death cry out, 'O for
a little more time, and O for the opportunities of
grace again! and O how shall I enter upon eternity
thus unprepared!' as if they had never heard or
known that they must die till now! Had you not a
life's time to put these questions, and should you not

long ago have got them satisfactorily resolved?
And justly doth God give over some to that greater
shame of human nature, as not to be called to their
wits, even by the approach of death itself, but as
they contemned everlasting life in their health, God
justly leaveth them to be so sottish, as to venture
presumptuously with unrenewed souls upon death,
and the conceit that they are of the right church, or
party, or opinion, or that the priest hath absolved
them, doth pass with them for the necessary preparation; and well were it for them if these would pass
them currently into heaven. But O what heart can
now conceive, how terrible it is for a new departed
soul to find itself remedilessly disappointed, and to be
shut up in flames and desperation, before they would
believe that they were in danger of it!

Reader, I beseech thee, as ever thou believest that
thou must shortly die, retire from the crowd and
noise of worldly vanity and vexation. O bethink
thee how little a while thou must be here, and have
use for honour, and favour, and wealth; and what
it is for a soul to pass into heaven or hell, and to
dwell among angels or devils for ever; and how men
should live, and watch, and pray, that are near to
such a change as this. Should I care what men call
me (by tongue or pen), should I care whether I live
at liberty or in prison, when I am ready to die, and
have matters of infinite moment before me, to take
me up? Honour, or dishonour, liberty or prison,
are words of no sound or signification scarce to be
heard or taken notice of, to one of us that are just
passing to God and to everlasting life. The Lord
have mercy upon the distracted world! How
strangely doth the devil befool them in the daylight,

and make them needlessly trouble themselves about many things, when one thing is needful! And heaven is talked of (and that but heartlessly and seldom) while fleshly provision only is the prize, the pleasure, the business of their lives! Some are diverted from their serious preparation for death, by the beastly avocations of lust and gaudiness, and meats, and drinks, and childish sports; and some by the businesses of ambition and covetousness, contriving how to feather their nests, and exercise their wills over others in the world; and some that will seem to be doing the work, are diverted as dangerously as others, by contending about formalities and ceremonies, and destroying charity and peace, rending the church, and strengthening factions, and carrying on interests hypocritically under the name of religion, till the *zeal* that *St. James* describeth, (James iii. 13, 14, &c.) having consumed all that was like to the *zeal of love and holiness* in themselves, proceed to consume the servants and interest of Christ about them, and to bite and devour, till their Lord come and find them in a day that they looked not for him, smiting their fellow-servants, and eating and drinking with the drunken, and cut them asunder, and appoint them their portion with the hypocrites, where shall be weeping and gnashing of teeth. (Matt. xxiv. 49—51.)

O study, and preach, and hear, and pray, and live, and use your brethren that differ from you in some opinions, as you would do if you were going to receive your doom, and as will then be most acceptable to your Lord! The guilt of sensuality, worldliness, ambition, of uncharitableness, cruelty and injustice, of losing time, and betraying your souls by negligence, or perfidiousness and wilful sin, will lie heavier upon a departing soul, than now in the drunkenness of prosperity you can think. Christ will never receive such souls in their extremity, unless upon repentance by faith in his blood, they are washed from this pollution. It is unspeakably terrible to die, without a confidence that Christ will receive us, and little knows the graceless world what sincerity and simplicity in holiness is necessary to the soundness of such a confidence.

Let those that know not that they must die, or know of no life hereafter, hold on their chace of a feather, till they find what they lost their lives, and souls, and labour for: but if thou be a Christian, remember what is thy work! Thou wilt not need the favour of man, nor worldly wealth to prevail with Christ to receive thy spirit. O learn thy last work, before thou art put upon the doing of it. The world of spirits to which we are passing, doth better know than this world of fleshly darkened sinners, the great difference between the death of a heavenly believer, and of an earthly sensualist. Believe it, it is a thing possible to get that apprehension of the love of Christ, that confidence of his receiving us, and such familiar, pleasant thoughts of our entertainment by him, as shall much overcome the fears of death, and make it a welcome day to us when we shall be admitted into the celestial society. And the difference between one man's death and another's, dependeth on the difference between heart and heart, life and life, preparation and unpreparedness.

If you ask me, How may so happy a preparation

be made? I have told you more fully elsewhere formerly. I shall add now these few Directions following.

1. *Follow the flattering world no further;* come off from all expectation of felicity below: *enjoy nothing under the sun;* but only use it in order to your enjoyment of the real sure delight. Take heed of being *too much pleased* in the creature. Have you houses, and lands, and offices, and honours, and friends that are very pleasing to you? Take heed; for that is the killing snare! Shut your eyes, and wink them all into nothing; and cast by your contrivances, and cares, and fears, and remember you have another work to do.

2. Live in communion with a suffering Christ; study well the whole life and nature of his sufferings; and the reason of them; and think how desirable it is to be conformed to him. Thus look to Jesus, that for the joy that was set before him, despised the shame, and endured the cross, and the contradiction of sinners against himself. Dwell upon this example, that the image of a humbled, suffering Christ being deeply imprinted on thy mind, may draw thy heart into a juster relish of a mortified state. Sure he is no good Christian that thinks it not better to live as Christ did, in holy poverty and sufferings in the world, than as *Crœsus* or *Cæsar*, or any such worldling and self-pleaser lived. Die daily, by following Jesus with your cross, and when you have awhile suffered with him, he will make you perfect, and receive your spirits, and you shall reign with him. It wonderfully prepareth for a comfortable death, to live in the fellowship of the sufferings of Christ: he

is most likely to die quietly, patiently and joyfully, that can first be poor, be neglected, be scorned, be wronged, be slandered, be imprisoned, quietly, patiently, and joyfully. If you were but at *Jerusalem,* you would with some love and pleasure go up *Mount Olivet,* and think, *Christ went this very way;* you would love to see the place where he was born, the way which he went when he carried his cross, the holy grave where he was buried, (where there is a temple which pilgrims use to visit, from whence they use to bring the mark as a pleasing badge of honour); but how much more of Christ is there in our suffering for his cause and truth; and in following him in a mortified, self-denying life, than in following him in the path that he hath trodden upon earth? His enemies saw his cross, his grave, his mother, his person; this did not heal their sinful souls and make them happy. But the cross that he calleth us to bear, is a life of suffering for righteousness sake, in which he commandeth us *to rejoice and be exceeding glad, because our reward is great in heaven, though all manner of evil be spoken of us falsely by men on earth;* Matt. v. 11, 12. This is called a *being partakers of Christ's sufferings,* in which we are commanded to rejoice; *that when this glory shall be revealed, we may be glad with exceeding joy;* 1 Pet. iv. 13. And as the *sufferings of Christ abound towards us, so will our consolation abound by Christ;* 1 Cor. i. 5. Till we come up to a life of willing mortification, and pleased contented suffering with Christ, we are in the lower form of his school, and as children, shall tremble at that which should not cause our terror, and through misapprehensions of the case of a departing soul, shall

be afraid of that which should be our joy.   I am not
such an enemy to the esteem of relics, but if one
could shew me the very *stocks* that *Paul* and *Silas* sat
in when they sung psalms in their imprisonment,
(Acts xvi,) I could be contented to be put (for the
like cause) into the same stocks, with a special willingness and pleasure : how much more should we
be willing to be conformed to our suffering Lord, in
a spirit and life of true mortification !

3. *Hold communion also with his suffering members.*
Desire not to dwell in *the tents of wickedness*, nor to
be planted among them that *flourish for a time, that
they may be destroyed for ever* ; Psal. xcii. 6, 7.   I had
rather have *Bradford's heart and faggot, than Bonner's
bishopric.*   It was holy *Stephen,* and not those that
stoned him, that saw heaven opened, and the Son of
Man sitting at the right hand of God, (Acts vii. 56,)
and that could joyfully say, *Lord Jesus, receive my spirit.*   He liveth not by faith (though he may be a
hanger-on that keepeth up some profession for fear
of being damned,) who *chooseth* not, *rather to suffer
affliction with the people of God, than to enjoy the pleasures of sin for a season, and esteemeth not the very
reproach of Christ greater riches than the treasures of
the world, as having respect to the recompence of reward*; Heb. xi. 25, 26.

4. *Live as if heaven were open to your sight ;* and
then doat upon the delights of worldlings if you can ;
then love a life of fleshly ease and honour better than
to be with Christ, if you can.   But of this I have
spoken at large in other writings.

Christian ! make it the study and business of thy
life, to learn to do thy *last work* well ; that *work*

which must be done but once; that so death which transmits unholy souls into utter darkness and despair, may deliver thy spirit into thy Redeemer's hands to be received to his glory, according to that blessed promise, John xii. 26; *If any man serve me, let him follow me: and where I am, there shall also my servant be : if any man serve me, him will my Father honour.*

APPENDIX :

CONTAINING

MR. BAXTER'S COMPARISON BETWEEN HIS YOUNGER AND
HIS RIPER YEARS; HIS SENTIMENTS ABOUT CONTROVER.
SIAL WRITINGS; HIS TEMPTATIONS AND DIFFICUL-
TIES; IMPROVEMENTS, DEFECTS, AND PENITENT·
CONFESSION OF HIS FAULTS.

BECAUSE it is soul-experiments which those that
urge me to this kind of writing, do expect that I
should especially communicate to others, and I have
said little of God's dealing with my soul since the
time of my younger years, I shall only give the reader
so much satisfaction, as to acquaint him truly what
change God hath made upon my mind and heart
since those unriper times, and wherein I now differ in
judgment and disposition from my [former] self: And
for any more particular account of heart-occurrences,
and God's operations on me, I think it somewhat
unsavory to recite them; seeing God's dealings are
much the same with all his servants in the main,
and the points wherein he varieth are usually so
small, that I think such not fit to be repeated: Nor
have I any thing extraordinary to glory in, which is
not common to the rest of my brethren, who have the
same Spirit, and are servants of the same Lord.
And the true reason why I do adventure so far upon
the censure of the world, as to tell them wherein the
case is altered with me, is that I may take off young

inexperienced Christians from being over-confident in their [first apprehensions, or overvaluing their first degrees of grace, or too much applauding and following unfurnished, inexperienced men; but may somewhat be directed what mind and course of life to prefer, by the judgment of one that hath tried both before them.

1 The temper of my *mind* hath somewhat altered with the temper of my *body*. When I was young, I was more *vigorous, affectionate, and fervent in preaching, conference and prayer*, than (ordinarily) I can be now; my style was more extempore and lax, but by the advantage of *affection*, and a very familiar, moving voice and utterance, my preaching then did more affect the auditory, than many of the last years before I gave over preaching; but yet what I delivered was much more raw, and had more passages that would not bear the trial of accurate judgments; and my discourses had both less *substance* and less *judgment* than of late.

2. My understanding was then quicker, and could more easily manage any thing that was newly presented to it upon a sudden; but it is since better furnished, and acquainted with the ways of truth and error, and with a multitude of particular mistakes of the world, which then I was the more in danger of, because I had only the *faculty* of knowing them, but did not *actually* know them. I was then like a man of a quick understanding that was to travel a way which he never went before, or to cast up an account which he never laboured in before, or to play on an instrument of music which he never saw before; and I am now like one of somewhat a slower understanding (by that *præmatura senectus* which weakness and

excessive bleedings brought me to) who is travelling a way which he hath often gone, and is casting up an account which he hath often cast up, and hath ready at hand, and that is playing on an instrument which he hath often played on; so that I can very confidently say, that my judgment is much sounder and firmer now than it was then; for though I am now as competent a judge of the *actings* of my own understanding then, yet I can judge of the *effects*: and when I peruse the writings which I wrote in my younger years, I can find the footsteps of my unfurnished mind, and of my emptiness and insufficiency: so that the man that followed my judgment then, was liker to have been misled by me, than he that should follow it now.

And yet, that I may not say worse than it deserveth of my former measure of understanding, I shall truly tell you what change I find now, in the perusal of my own writings. Those points which then I *thoroughly studied,* my judgment is the same of *now* as it was *then;* and therefore in the *substance* of my religion, and in those controversies which I then searched into, with some extraordinary diligence, I find not my mind disposed to a change: But in divers points that I studied slightly and by the halves, and in many things which I took upon trust from others, I have found since that my apprehensions were either erroneous or very lame. And those things which I was orthodox in, I had either insufficient reasons for, or a mixture of some sound and some insufficient ones, or else an insufficient apprehension of those reasons; so that I scarcely knew what I seemed to know. And though in my writings I found little in substance which my present judgment differeth from, yet in my

Aphorisms and *Saints' Rest* (which were my first writings) I find some raw, unmeet expressions; and one common infirmity I perceive, that I put off matters with some kind of confidence, as if I had done something new or more than ordinary in them, when upon my more mature reviews, I find that I said not half that which the subject did require; as *e. g.* in the doctrine of the Covenants, and of Justification, but especially about the divine authority of the Scripture in the second part of the *Saints' Rest;* where I have not said half that should have been said; and the reason was, because that I had not read any of the fuller sort of books that are written on those subjects, nor conversed with those that knew more than myself, and so all those things were either new or great to me, which were common and small perhaps to others; and because they all came in by the way of my own study of the naked matter, and not from books, they were apt to affect my mind the more, and to seem greater than they were. And this token of my weakness accompanied those my younger studies, that I was very apt to start up controversies in the way of my practical writings, and also more desirous to acquaint the world with all that I took to be the truth, and to assault those books by name which I thought did tend to deceive them, and did contain unsound and dangerous doctrine. And the reason of all this was, that I was then in the vigour of my youthful apprehensions, and the new appearance of any sacred truth, it was more apt to affect me, and to be more highly valued, than afterward, when commonness had dulled my delight; and I did not sufficiently discern then how much in most of our controversies is verbal, and upon mutual mistakes.

And withal I knew not how impatient divines were of being contradicted, nor how it would stir up all their powers to defend what they have once said, and to rise up against the truth which is thus thrust upon them, as the mortal enemy of their honour: and I knew not how hardly men's minds are changed from their former apprehensions be the evidence never so plain. And I have perceived, that nothing so much hindereth the reception of the truth, as urging it on men with too harsh importunity, and falling too heavily on their errors: for hereby you engage their honour in the business, and they defend their errors as themselves, and stir up all their wit and ability to oppose you. In controversies it is fierce opposition which is the bellows to kindle a resisting zeal; when if they be neglected, and their opinions lie awhile despised, they usually cool and come again to themselves; (though I know that this holdeth not when the greediness and increase of his followers, doth animate a sectary, even though he have no opposition.) Men are so loath to be drenched with the truth, that I am no more for going that way to work; and to confess the truth, I am lately much prone to the *contrary extreme*, to be too indifferent what men hold, and to keep my judgment to myself, and never to mention any thing wherein I differ from another, or any thing which I think I know more than he; or at least, if he receive it not presently to silence it, and leave him to his own opinion: and I find this effect is mixed according to its causes, which are some *good*, and some *bad*. The *bad causes* are, 1. An impatience of men's weakness and mistaking frowardness and self-conceitedness. 2. An abatement of my *sensible* esteem of *truth*, through the long abode

of them on my mind: though 'my judgment value
them, yet it is hard to be equally *affected* with old
and common things, as with *new* and *rare* ones.
The better causes are, 1. That I am much more sensible than ever of the necessity of living upon the
principles of religion, which we are all agreed in, and
uniting these: and how much mischief men 'that
overvalue their own opinions have done by their *controversies* in the church; how some have destroyed
charity, and some caused schisms by them, and most
have hindered godliness in themselves and others,
and used them to divert men from the serious prose-
cuting of a holy life; and as *Sir Francis Bacon* saith,
in his *Essay of Peace,* that it is one great benefit of
church-peace and concord, that writing controversies
is turned into books of practical devotion for increase
of piety and virtue. 2. And I find that it is much
more for most men's good and edification, to converse
with them only in that way of godliness which all are
agreed in, and not by touching upon differences to
stir up their corruptions; and to tell them of little
more of your knowledge, than what you find them
willing to receive from you as mere learners; and
therefore to stay till they *crave* information of you,
(as *Musculus* did with the Anabaptists, when he visited them in prison, and conversed kindly and
lovingly with them, and shewed them all the love he
could, and never talked to them of their opinions,
till at last they who were wont to call him a deceiver,
and false prophet, did entreat him to instruct them,
and received his instructions.) We mistake men's
diseases when we think there needeth nothing to
cure their errors, but only to bring them the *evidence*
of truth: alas! there are many distempers of mind

to be removed, before men are apt to *receive* that evidence. And therefore that church is happy where order is kept up, and the abilities of the ministers command a reverend submission from the hearers; and where all are in Christ's school in the distinct ranks of teachers and learners : for in a learning way men are ready to receive the truth, but in a disputing way they come armed against it with prejudice and animosity.

3. And I must say farther, that what I last mentioned on the by, is one of the most notable changes of my mind. In my youth I was quickly past my fundamentals, and was running up into a multitude of controversies, and greatly delighted with metaphysical and scholastic writings, (though I must needs say, my preaching was still on the necessary points); but the older I grew the smaller stress I laid upon these controversies and curiosities, (though still my intellect abhorreth confusion,) as finding far greater uncertainties in them, than I at first discerned, and finding less *usefulness* comparatively, even where there is the greatest certainty. And now it is the fundamental doctrines of the Catechism, which I most highly value, and daily think of, and find most useful to myself and others. The Creed, the Lord's-prayer, and the Ten Commandments, do find me now the most acceptable and plentiful matter for all my meditations; they are to me as my daily bread and drink : and as I can speak and write of them over and over again, so I had rather read or hear of them, than of any of the school niceties, which once so much pleased me. And thus I observed it was with old *Bishop Usher*, and with many other men;

and I conjecture that this effect also is mixed of *good* and *bad*, according to its causes.

The *bad cause* may perhaps be some natural infirmity or decay : and as trees in the spring shoot up into branches, leaves and blossoms, but in the autumn the life draws down into the root, so possibly, my nature, conscious of its infirmity and decay, may find itself insufficient for numerous particles, and assurgency to the attempting of difficult things ; and so my mind may retire to the root of Christian principles ; and also I have been often afraid, lest ill-rooting at first, and many temptations afterwards, have made it more necessary for me than many others to retire to the root, and secure my fundamentals. But upon much observation I am afraid lest most others are in no better a case ; and that at the first they take it for a granted thing, that Christ is the Saviour of the world, and that the soul is immortal, and that there is a heaven and a hell, &c., while they are studying abundance of scholastic superstructures, and at last will find cause to study more soundly their religion itself, as well as I have done.

The *better* causes are these : 1. I value all things according to their *use* and *ends* ; and I find in the daily practice and experience of my soul, that the knowledge of God, and Christ, and the Holy Spirit, and the truth of Scripture, and the life to come, and of a holy life, is of *more use* to me, than all the most curious speculations. 2. I know that every man must grow (as trees do) downwards and upwards both at once ; and that the *roots* increase as the bulk and branches do. 3. Being nearer death and another world, I am the more regardful of those things

which my everlasting life or death depend on. 4.
Having most to do with ignorant, miserable people,
I am commanded by my charity and reason, to treat
with them of that which their salvation lieth on ; and
not to dispute with them of formalities and niceties,
when the question is presently to be determined whether they shall dwell for ever in heaven or in hell.
In a word, my *meditations* must be most upon the
matters of my practice and my interest : and as the
love of God, and the seeking of everlasting life is the
matter of my *practice* and my *interest*, so must it be
of my meditation. That is the *best* doctrine and study which maketh men *better*, and tendeth to make
them *happy*. I abhor the folly of those unlearned
persons, who revile or despise learning because they
know not what it is : and I take not any piece of
true learning to be useless : and yet my soul appro-
veth of the resolution of holy *Paul*, who determined
to know nothing among his hearers, (that is, comparatively to value and make ostentation of no other
wisdom) but (the knowledge of) a crucified Christ ;
to know God in Christ is life eternal. As the stock
of the tree affordeth timber to build houses and cities, when the small though higher multifarious
branches are but to make a crow's nest or a blaze,
so the knowledge of God and of Jesus Christ, of heaven and holiness, doth build up the soul to endless
blessedness, and affordeth it solid peace and comfort,
when a multitude of school niceties serve but for vain
janglings, and hurtful diversions and contentions.
And yet I would not dissuade my reader from the
perusal of *Aquinas, Scotus, Ockham, Arminiensis, Du-
randus,* or any such writer, for much good may be
gotten from them : but I would persuade him to stu-

dy and live upon the essential doctrines of Christianity and godliness, incomparably above them all. And that he may know that my testimony is somewhat regardable, I presume to say, that in this I as much gainsay my natural inclination •to subtlety and accurateness in knowing, as he is like to do by his, if he obey my counsel. And I think if he lived among infidels and enemies of Christ, he would find that to make good the *doctrine of faith* and of *life eternal*, were not only his noblest and most useful study, but also that which would require the height of all his parts, and the utmost of his diligence, to manage it skilfully to the satisfaction of himself and others.

4. I add therefore that this is another thing which I am changed in ; that whereas in my younger days I never was tempted to doubt of the truth of Scripture or Christianity, but all my doubts and fears were exercised at home, about my own sincerity and interest in Christ, and this was it which I called *unbelief;* since then my sorest assaults have been on the other side, and such they were, that had I been void of internal experience, and the adhesion of love, and the special help of God, and had not discerned more reason for my religion than I did when I was younger, I had certainly apostatized to infidelity, (though for *atheism* or *ungodliness*, my reason seeth no stronger arguments, than may be brought to prove that there is no earth, or air, or sun.) I am now therefore much more apprehensive than heretofore of the necessity of well grounding men in their religion, and especially of the witness of the indwelling Spirit ; for I more sensibly perceive that the *Spirit* is the great witness of Christ and Christianity to the world : and though the folly of fanatics tempted me long to over-

look the strength of this testimony of the Spirit, while they placed it in a certain *internal assertion,* or enthusiastic inspiration ; yet now I see that the Holy Ghost in another manner is the witness of Christ and his agent in the world. The Spirit in the prophets was his first witness ; and the Spirit by miracles was the second ; and the Spirit by renovation, sanctifica- tion, illumination and consolation, assimilating the soul to Christ and heaven is the continued witness to all true believers ; and if any man have not the Spi- rit of Christ, the same is none of his ; Rom: viii. 9. Even as the rational soul in the child is the inherent witness or evidence, that he is the child of rational parents. And therefore ungodly persons have a great disadvantage in their resisting temptations to unbe- lief, and it is no wonder if Christ be a *stumbling-block* to the Jews, and to the Gentiles foolishness. There is many a one that hideth his temptations to infideli- ty, because he thinketh it a shame to open them, and because it may generate doubts in others ; but I doubt the imperfection of most men's care of their salvation, and of their diligence and resolution in a holy life, doth come from the imperfection of their belief of Christianity and the life to come. For my part I must profess, that when my belief of things eternal and of the Scripture is most clear and firm, all goeth accordingly in my soul, and all temptations to sinful compliances, worldliness or flesh-pleasing, do signify worse to me, than an invitation to the stocks or bedlam : and no petition seemeth more ne- cessary to me, than, *Lord, increase our faith ; I be- lieve, help thou my unbelief.*

5. Among truths certain in themselves, all are not equally certain unto me ; and even of the mysteries of the Gospel, I must needs say with *Mr. Richard*

H

Hooker (Eccles. Polit.), that whatever men may pretend, the subjective certainty cannot go beyond the objective evidence; for it is caused thereby as the print on the wax is caused by that on the seal: therefore I do more of late than ever discern a necessity of a methodical procedure in maintaining the doctrine of Christianity, and of beginning at natural verities, as presupposed fundamentally to supernatural, (though God may when he please reveal all at once, and even natural truths by supernatural revelation): and it is a marvellous great help to my faith, to find it built on so sure foundations, and so consonant to the law of nature. I am not so foolish as to pretend my certainty to be greater than it is, merely because it is a dishonour to be less certain; nor will I by shame be kept from confessing those infirmities, which those have as much as I, who hypocritically reproach me with them. My certainty that I am a man, is before my certainty that there is a God, for *quod facit notum est magis notum:* my certainty that there is a God, is greater than my certainty that he requireth love and holiness of his creature: my certainty of *this* is greater than my certainty of the life of reward and punishment hereafter: my certainty of that is greater than my certainty of the endless duration of it, and of the immortality of individuate souls: my certainty of the Deity is greater than my certainty of the Christian faith: my certainty of the Christian faith in its essentials, is greater than my certainty of the perfection and infallibility of all the Holy Scriptures: my certainty of that is greater than my certainty of the meaning of many particular texts, and so of the truth of many particular doctrines, and of the canonicalness of some certain books. So that as you see by what gradations my understanding doth proceed, so also that my certainty differeth as the evidences differ. And they that have attained to greater perfection, and a higher degree of certainty than I, should pity me and produce their evidence to help me. And they that will begin all their certainty with that of the truth of the Scripture, as the *principium cognoscendi*, may meet me at the same end; but they must give me leave to undertake to prove to a heathen or infidel, the being of a God, and the necessity of holiness, and the certainty of a reward or punishment, even while he yet denieth the truth of Scripture, and in order to his believing it to be true.

6. In my younger years, my trouble for sin was most about my actual failings in thought, word or action, (except hardness of heart, of which more anon). But now I am much more troubled for inward defects, and omission or want of the vital duties or graces in the soul. My daily trouble is so much for my ignorance of God, and weakness of belief, and want of greater love to God, and strangeness to him, and to the life to come, and for want of a greater willingness to die, and longing to be with God in heaven, as that I take not some immoralities, though very great, to be in themselves so great and odious sins, if they could be found as separate from these. Had I all the riches of the world, how gladly should I give them, for a fuller knowledge, belief, and love of God and everlasting glory! These wants are the greatest burden of my life, which oft maketh my life itself a burden. And I cannot find any hope of reaching so high in these, while I am in the flesh, as I once hoped before this time to have attained; which maketh me the wearier of this sinful world, which is honoured with so little of the knowledge of God.

7. Heretofore I placed much of my religion in ten-

derness of heart, and grieving for sin, and penitential tears; and less of it in the love of God, and studying his love and goodness, and in his joyful praises, than now I do. Then I was little sensible of the greatness and excellency of love and praise; though I coldly spake the same words in its commendations, as now I do; and now I am less troubled for want of grief and tears, (though I more value humility, and refuse not needful humiliation): but my conscience now looketh at love and delight in God, and praising him, as the top of all my religious duties, for which it is that I value and use the rest.

8. My judgment is much more for frequent and serious meditation on the heavenly blessedness, than it was heretofore in my younger days. I then thought that a sermon of the attributes of God, and the joys of heaven were not the most excellent; and was wont to say, 'Every body knoweth this, that God is great, and good, and that heaven is a blessed place; I had rather hear how I may attain it.' And nothing pleased me so well as the doctrine of Regeneration, and the marks of sincerity; which was because it was suitable to me in that state: but now I had rather read, hear or meditate on God and heaven, than on any other subject: for I perceive that it is the object that altereth and elevateth the mind, which will be such as that is, which it most frequently feedeth on: and that it is not only useful to our comfort, to be much in heaven in our believing thoughts, but that it must animate all our other duties, and fortify us against every temptation and sin; and that the love of the end is it that is the poise or spring, which setteth every wheel a-going, and must put us on to all the means: and that a man is no more a Christian indeed than he is heavenly.

9. I was once wont to meditate most on my own heart, and to dwell all at home, and look little higher; I was still poring either on my sins or wants, or examining my sincerity; but now though I am greatly convinced of the need of heart-acquaintance and employment, yet I see more need of a higher work; and that I should look oftener upon Christ, and God, and heaven, than upon my own heart. At home I can find distempers to trouble me, and some evidences of my peace; but it is above that I must find matter of delight and joy, and love, and peace itself. Therefore I would have one thought at home upon myself and sins, and many thoughts above, upon the high and amiable and beatifying objects.

10. Heretofore I knew much less than now, and yet was not half so much acquainted with my ignorance: I had a great delight in the daily new discoveries which I made, and of the light which shined in upon me, (like a man that cometh into a country where he never was before): but I little knew either how imperfectly I understood those very points, whose discovery so much delighted me, nor how much might be said against them; nor how many things I was yet a stranger to: but now I find far greater darkness upon all things, and perceive how very little it is that we know in comparison of that which we are ignorant of, and have far meaner thoughts of my own understanding, though I must needs know that it is better furnished than it was then.

11. Accordingly I had then a far higher opinion of learned persons and books, than I have now; for what I wanted myself, I thought every reverend divine had attained, and was familiarly acquainted with: and what books I understood not by reason of the strangeness of the terms or matter, I the more

admired and thought that others understood their worth. But now experience hath constrained me against my will to know, that reverend learned men are imperfect, and know but little as well as I ; especially those that think themselves the wisest : and the better I am acquainted with them, the more I perceive that we are all yet in the dark : and the more I am acquainted with holy men, that are all for heaven, and pretend not much to subtleties, the more I value and honour them. And when I have studied hard to understand some abstruse admired book, as *De Scientia Dei, De Providentia circa malum, de Decretis, de Predeterminatione, de Libertate Creaturæ, &c.* I have but attained the knowledge of human imperfection, and to see that the author is but a man as well as I.

12. And at first I took more upon my author's credit, than now I can do : and when an author was highly commended to me by others, or pleased me in some part, I was ready to entertain the whole ; whereas now I take and leave in the same author, and dissent in some things from him that I like best, as well as from others.

13. At first I was greatly inclined to go with the *highest* in controversies, on one side or other ; as with *Dr. Twisse,* and *Mr. Rutherford,* and *Spanhemius de Providentia et Gratia, &c.* But now I can so easily see what to say against both extremes, that I am much more inclinable to reconciling principles. And whereas then I thought that conciliators were but ignorant men, that were willing to please all, and would pretend to reconcile the world by principles which they did not understand themselves ; I have since perceived that if the amiableness of peace and concord had no hand in the business, yet greater light and stronger judgment usually is with the reconcilers,

than with either of the contending parties, (as with *Davenant, Hall, Usher, Lud. Crocius, Berglus, Strangius, Camero, &c.)* But on both accounts their writings are most acceptable, though I know that moderation may be a pretext of errors.

14. At first the style of authors took as much with me as the argument, and made the arguments seem more forcible: but now I judge not of truth at all by any such ornaments or accidents, but by its naked evidence.

15. I now see more *good* and more *evil* in all men than heretofore I did: I see that *good* men are not so *good*, as I once thought they were, but have more imperfections; and that nearer approach and fuller trial, doth make the best appear more weak and faulty, than their admirers at a distance think. And I find that few are so bad, as either their malicious enemies, or censorious, separating professors do imagine. In some indeed I find that human nature is corrupted into a greater likeness to devils, than I once thought any on earth had been. But even in the wicked usually there is more for grace to make advantage of, and more to testify for God and holiness, than I once believed there had been.

16. I less admire *gifts of utterance* and *bare profession* of religion than I once did; and have much more charity for many, who by the want of gifts, do make a more obscure profession than they. I once thought that almost all that could pray movingly and fluently, and talk well of religion had been saints. But experience hath opened to me, what odious crimes may consist with high profession; and I have met with divers obscure persons, not noted for any extraordinary profession, or forwardness in religion, but only to live a quiet, blameless life, whom I have after

found to have long lived, as far as I could discern, a truly godly and sanctified life; only their prayers and duties were by accident kept secret from other men's observation. Yet he that upon this pretence would confound the godly and the ungodly, may as well go about to lay heaven and hell together.

17. I am not so narrow in my *special love* as heretofore: being less censorious, and talking more than I did for saints, it must needs follow that I love more as saints than I did before. 1 think it not lawful to put that man off with bare church-communion, and such common love which I must allow the wicked, who professeth himself a true Christian, by such a profession as I cannot disprove.

18. I am not so narrow in my principles of church-communion as once I was: I more plainly perceive the difference between the church as congregate or visible, and as regenerate or mystical; and between sincerity and profession; and that a credible profession is proof sufficient of a man's title to church-admission; and that the profession is credible *in foro Ecclesiæ*, which is not disproved. I am not for narrowing the church more than Christ himself alloweth us, nor for robbing him of any of his flock. I am more sensible how much it is the will of Christ that every man be the chooser or refuser of his own felicity, and that it lieth most on his own hands, whether he will have communion with the church or not, and that if he be an hypocrite it is himself that will bear the loss.

19. Yet am I more apprehensive than ever of the great use and need of ecclesiastical discipline, and what a sin it is in the pastors of the church, to make no more distinction, but by bare names and sacraments, and to force all the unmeet against their own

wills, to church-communion and sacraments, (though the ignorant and erroneous may sometimes be forced to hear instruction) : and what a great dishonour to Christ it is, when the church shall be as vicious as Pagan and Mahometan assemblies, and shall differ from them only in ceremony and name.

20. I am much more sensible of the evil of schism, and of the separating humour, and of gathering parties, and making several sects in the church than I was heretofore. For the effects have shewed us more of the mischiefs.

21. I am much more sensible how prone many young professors are to spiritual pride and self-conceitedness, and unruliness and division, and so to prove the grief of their teachers, and firebrands in the church ; and how much of a minister's work lieth in preventing this, and humbling and confirming such young, inexperienced professors, and keeping them in order in their progress in religion.

22. Yet am I more sensible of the sin and mischief of using men cruelly in matters of religion, and of pretending men's good, and the order of the church, for acts of inhumanity or uncharitableness : such know not their own infirmity, nor yet the nature of pastoral government, which ought to be paternal and by love; nor do they know the way to win a soul, nor to maintain the church's peace.

23. My soul is much more afflicted with the thoughts of the miserable world, and more drawn out in desire of their conversion than heretofore ; I was wont to look but little further than *England* in my prayers, as not considering the state of the rest of the world ; or if I prayed for the conversion of the Jews, that was almost all. But now, as I better understand the case of the world, and the method of the

Lord's-prayer, so there is nothing in the world that lieth so heavy upon my heart, as the thought of the miserable nations of the earth. It is the most astonishing part of all God's providence to me, that he so far forsaketh almost all the world, and confineth his special favour to so few; that so small a part of the world hath the profession of Christianity, in comparison of Heathens, Mahometans, and other infidels! And that among professed Christians there are so few that are saved from gross delusions, and have but any competent knowledge; and that among *those* there are so few that are seriously religious, and truly set their hearts on heaven. I cannot be affected so much with the calamities of my own relations, or the land of my nativity, as with the case of the Heathen, Mahometan, and ignorant nations of the earth. No part of my prayers are so deeply serious, as that for the conversion of the infidel and ungodly world, that God's name may be sanctified, and his kingdom come, and his will be done on earth as it is in heaven: nor was I ever before so sensible what a plague the division of languages was, which hindereth our speaking to them for their conversion; nor what a great sin tyranny is, which keepeth out the Gospel from most of the nations of the world. Could we but go among Tartarians, Turks, and Heathens, and speak their language, I should be but little troubled for the silencing of eighteen hundred ministers at once in *England,* nor for all the rest that were cast out here, and in *Scotland* and *Ireland:* there being no employment in the world so desirable in my eyes, as to labour for the winning of such miserable souls; which maketh me greatly honour *Mr. John Elliot,* the apostle of the Indians in *New England,* and whoever else have laboured in such work.

24. Yet am I not so much inclined to pass a peremptory sentence of damnation upon all that never heard of Christ; having some more reason than I knew of before, to think that God's dealing with such is much unknown to *us*; and that the ungodly here, among us Christians, are in a far worse case than they.

25. My censures of the Papists do much differ from what they were at first: I then thought that their errors in the doctrines of faith were their most dangerous mistakes, as in the points of merit, justification by works, assurance of salvation, the nature of faith, &c. But now I am assured that their mis-expressions, and misunderstanding us, with our mistakings of them, and inconvenient expressing our own opinions, hath made the difference in these points to appear much greater than they are; and that in some of them it is next to none at all. But the great and unreconcilable differences lie, in their church tyranny and usurpations, and in their great corruptions and abasement of God's worship, together with their befriending of ignorance and vice. At first I thought that *Mr. Perkins* well proved that a Papist cannot go beyond a reprobate: but now I doubt not but that God hath many sanctified ones among them, who have received the true doctrine of Christianity so practically, that their contradictory errors prevail not against them, to hinder their love of God and their salvation; but that their errors are like a conquerable dose of poison which nature doth overcome. And I can never believe that a man may not be saved by that religion, which doth but bring him to the true love of God, and to a heavenly mind and life; nor that God will ever cast a soul into hell that truly loveth him. Also at first it would disgrace any doctrine with me, if I did but hear it called Popery and

Antichristian; but I have long learned to be more impartial, and to dislike men for bad doctrine, rather than the doctrines for the men : and to know that Satan can use even the names of Popery and Antichrist, against a truth.

26. I am more deeply afflicted for the disagreements of Christians than I was when I was a younger Christian. Except the case of the Infidel world, nothing is so sad and grievous to my thoughts, as the case of the divided churches. And therefore I am more deeply sensible of the sinfulness of those prelates and pastors of the churches, who are the principal cause of these divisions. O how many millions of souls are kept by them in ignorance and ungodliness, and deluded by faction, as if it were true religion. How is the conversion of infidels hindered by them ; and Christ and religion heinously dishonoured ! The contentions between the Greek church and the Roman, the Papists and the Protestants, the Lutherans and the Calvinists, have woefully hindered the kingdom of Christ.

27. I have spent much of my studies about the terms of Christian concord, and have over and over considered of the several ways, which several sorts of reconcilers have devised. I have thought of the Papist's way, who think there will be no union, but by coming over wholly to their church: and I have found that it is neither possible nor desirable. I have thought and thought again of the way of the moderating Papists, *Cassander, Grotius, Baldwin, &c.,* and of those that would have all reduced to the state of the times of *Gregory the First,* before the division of the Greek and Latin churches, that the Pope might have his primacy, and govern all the church by the canons of the Councils, with a *salvo* to the rights of

kings, and patriarchs, and prelates ; and that the doctrines and worship which then were received might
prevail. And for my own part, if I lived in such a
state of the church, I would live peaceably, as glad of
unity, though lamenting the corruption and tyranny ;
but I am fully assured that none of these are the true,
desirable terms of unity, nor such as are ever likely to
procure a universal concord : and I am as sure that the
true means and terms of concord are obvious and easy
to an impartial mind. And that these three things
alone would easily heal and unite all the churches.

(1.) That all Christian princes and governors take
all the coercive power about religion into their own
hands, (though if prelates and their courts must be
used as their officers in exercising that coercive power,
so be it) : and that they make a difference between
the approved and the tolerated churches ; and that
they keep the peace between these churches, and settle
their several privileges by a law.

(2.) That the churches be accounted tolerable, who
profess all that is in the Creed, Lord's Prayer and
Decalogue in particular, and generally all that they
shall find to be revealed in the Word of God, and
hold communion in teaching, prayer, praises, and the
two Sacraments, not obstinately preaching any heresy
contrary to the particular articles which they profess,
nor seditiously disturbing the public peace : and that
such heretical preaching, and such seditious unpeaceableness, or notorious wickedness of life, do forfeit
their toleration.

(3.) And that those that are further orthodox in
those particulars, which rulers think fit to impose
upon their subjects, have their public maintenance
and greater encouragement. Yea, and this much is
become necessary, but upon supposition that men will

still be so self-conceited and uncharitable, as not to forbear their unnecessary impositions. Otherwise there would be found but very few who are *tolerable*, that are not also in their measure to be approved, maintained and encouraged. And if the primitive simplicity in doctrine, government and worship, might serve turn for the terms of the churches' union and communion, all would be well without any more ado; supposing that where Christian magistrates are, they keep the peace, and repress the offenders, and exercise all the coercive government : and heretics, who will subscribe to the Christian faith, must not be punished because they will subscribe to no more, but because they are proved to preach or promote heresy, contrary to the faith which they profess.

28. I am farther than ever I was from expecting great matters of unity, splendor or prosperity to the church on earth, or that saints should dream of a kingdom of this world, or flatter themselves with the hopes of a golden age, or reigning over the ungodly, (till there be " a new heaven and a new earth wherein dwelleth righteousness"). And on the contrary I am more apprehensive that sufferings must be the churches' most ordinary lot, and Christians indeed must be self-denying cross-bearers, even where there are none but formal, nominal Christians to be the cross-makers. And though ordinarily God would have vicissitudes of summer and winter, day and night, that the church may grow extensively in the summer of prosperity, and intensively and radically in the winter of adversity ; yet usually their night is longer than their day, and that day itself hath its storms and tempests. For the prognostics are evident in their causes : 1. The church will be still imperfect and sinful, and will have those diseases which

need this bitter remedy. 2. Rich men will be the rulers of the world; and rich men will be generally so far from true godliness, that they must come to heaven as by human impossibilities, as a camel through a needle's eye. 3. The ungodly will ever have an enmity against the image of God, and he that is born of the flesh will persecute him that is born after the Spirit; and brotherhood will not keep a Cain from killing an Abel who offereth a more acceptable sacrifice than himself; and the guilty will still hate the light, and make a prey to their pride and malice of a conscionable reprover. 4. The pastors will be still troubling the church with their pride, and avarice, and contentions; and the worst will be seeking to be the greatest, and they that seek it are likest to attain it. 5. He that is highest will be still imposing his conceits upon those under him, and lording it over God's heritage, and with Diotrephes casting out the brethren, and ruling them by constraint, and not as volunteers. 6. Those that are truly judicious will still comparatively be few; and consequently the troublers and dividers will be the multitude; and a judicious peacemaker and reconciler will be neglected, slighted, or hated by both extremes. 7. The tenor of the Gospel predictions, precepts, promises and threatenings, are fitted to a people in a suffering state. 8. And the graces of God in a believer are mostly suited to a state of suffering. 9. Christians must imitate Christ, and suffer with him before they reign with him; and his kingdom was not of this world. 10. The observation of God's dealing hitherto with the church in every age confirmeth me: and his befooling them that have dreamed of glorious times. It was such dreams that transported the Munster Anabaptists, and the followers of David George in the

Low Countries, and Campanella, and the Illuminati among the Papists, and our English Anabaptists and other fanatics here, both in the army and the city and country. When they think the golden age is come, they shew their dreams in their extravagant actions : and as our Fifth Monarchy men, they are presently upon some unquiet, rebellious attempt, to set up Christ in his kingdom whether he will or not. I remember how Abraham Scultetus in *Curriculo Vitæ suæ*, confesseth the common vanity of himself and other Protestants in Germany, who seeing the princes in England, France, Bohemia, and many other countries to be all at once both great and wise, and friends to reformation, did presently expect the golden age : but within one year either death, or ruins of war, or backslidings, had exposed all their expectations to scorn, and laid them lower than before.

29. I do not lay so great a stress upon the external modes and forms of worship as many young professors do. I have suspected myself, as perhaps the reader may do, that this is from a cooling and declining from my former zeal (though the truth is, I never much complied with men of that mind) ; but I find that judgment and charity are the causes of it, as far as I am able to discover. I cannot be so narrow in my principles of church-communion as many are, that are so much for a liturgy, or so much against it, so much for ceremonies or so much against them, that they can hold communion with no church that is not of their mind and way. If I were among the Greeks, the Lutherans, the Independents, yea, the Anabaptists (that own no heresy, nor set themselves against charity and peace), I would hold sometimes occasional communion with them as Christians, (if they will give me leave, without forcing me to any

sinful subscription or action): though my most usual communion should be with that society which I thought most agreeable to the Word of God, if I were free to choose. I cannot be of their opinion that think God will not accept him that prayeth by the Common Prayer Book, and that such forms are a self-invented worship which God rejecteth : nor yet can I be of their mind that say the like of extemporary prayers.

30. I am much less regardful of the approbation of man, and set much lighter by contempt or applause than I did long ago. I am oft suspicious that this is not only from the increase of self-denial and humility ; but partly from my being glutted and surfeited with human applause : and all worldly things appear most vain and unsatisfactory when we have tried them most. But though I feel that this hath some hand in the effect, yet as far as I can perceive, the knowledge of man's nothingness, and God's transcendent greatness, with whom it is that I have most to do, and the sense of the brevity of human things, and the nearness of eternity are the principal causes of this effect, which some have imputed to self-conceitedness and morosity.

31. I am more and more pleased with a solitary life ; and though in a way of self-denial I could submit to the most public life for the service of God, when he requireth it, and would not be unprofitable that I might be private; yet I must confess, it is much more pleasing to myself to be retired from the world, and to have very little to do with men, and to converse with God, and conscience, and good books; of which I have spoken my heart in my " Divine Life," Part III.

32. Though I was never much tempted to the sin of covetousness, yet my fear of dying was wont to tell me, that I was not sufficiently loosened from this

world. But I find that it is comparatively very easy to me to be loose from this world, but hard to live by faith above. To despise earth is easy to me; but not so easy to be acquainted and conversant in heaven. I have nothing in this world which I could not easily let go; but to get satisfying apprehensions of the other world is the great and grievous difficulty.

33. I am much more apprehensive than long ago, of the odiousness and danger of the sin of pride; scarce any sin appeareth more odious to me: having daily more acquaintance with the lamentable naughtiness and frailty of man, and of the mischiefs of that sin, and especially in matters spiritual and ecclesiastical. I think so far as any man is proud he is kin to the devil, and utterly a stranger to God and to himself. It is a wonder that it should be a possible sin to men that still carry about with them, in soul and body, such humbling matter of remedy as we all do.

34. I more than ever lament the unhappiness of the nobility, gentry, and great ones of the world, who live in such temptation to sensuality, curiosity, and wasting of their time about a multitude of little things; and whose lives are too often the transcript of the sins of Sodom, pride, fulness of bread, and abundance of idleness, and want of compassion to the poor. And I more value the life of the poor labouring man; but especially of him that hath neither poverty nor riches.

35. I am much more sensible than heretofore, of the breadth, and length, and depth of the radical, universal, odious sin of selfishness, and therefore have written so much against it; and of the excellency and necessity of self-denial, and of a public mind, and of loving our neighbours as ourselves.

36. I am more and more sensible that most controversies have more need of right stating than of de-

bating; and if my skill be increased in any thing, it is in that, in narrowing controversies by explication, and separating the *real* from the *verbal*, and proving to many contenders that they differ less than they think they do.

37. I am more solicitous than I have been about my duty to God, and less solicitous about his dealings with me, as being assured that he will do all things well; and as acknowledging the goodness of all the declarations of his holiness, even in the punishment of man; and as knowing that there is no rest but in the will and goodness of God.

38. Though my works were never such as could be any temptation to me to dream of obliging God by proper merit, in commutative justice; yet one of the most ready, constant, undoubted evidences of my uprightness and interest in his covenant, is the consciousness of my living as devoted to him. And I the more easily believe the pardon of my failings through my Redeemer, while I know that I serve no other master, and that I know no other end, or trade, or business; but that I am employed in his work, and make it the business of my life, and live to him in the world notwithstanding my infirmities. And this bent and business of my life, with my longing desires after perfection, in the knowledge, and belief and love of God, and in a holy and heavenly mind and life, are the two standing, constant, discernible evidences which most put me out of doubt of my sincerity: and I find that constant action and duty is it that keepeth the first always in sight; and constant wants and weaknesses, and coming short of my desires, do make those desires still the more troublesome, and so the more easily still perceived.

39. Though my habitual judgment, and resolution,

and scope of life be still the same, yet I find a great mutability as to actual apprehensions, and degrees of grace; and consequently find that so mutable a thing as the mind of man would never keep itself if God were not its keeper. When I have been seriously musing upon the reasons of Christianity, with the concurrent evidences methodically placed in their just advantages before my eyes, I am so clear in my belief of the Christian verities, that Satan hath little room for a temptation. But sometimes when he hath on a sudden set some temptation before me, when the aforesaid evidences have been out of the way, or less upon my thoughts, he hath by such surprises amazed me, and weakened my faith in the present act. So also as to the love of God, and trusting in him, sometimes when the motives are clearly apprehended, the duty is more easy and delightful: and at other times I am merely passive and dull, if not guilty of actual despondency and distrust.

40. I am much more cautelous in my belief of history than heretofore: not that I run into their extreme that will believe nothing because they cannot believe all things. But I am abundantly satisfied by the experience of this age, that there is no believing two sorts of men, *ungodly* men, and *partial* men; though an honest heathen of no religion may be believed, where enmity against religion biasseth him not; yet a debauched Christian, besides his enmity to the power and practice of his own religion, is seldom without some farther bias of interest or faction; especially when these concur, and a man is both ungodly and ambitious, espousing an interest contrary to a holy, heavenly life; and also factious, embodying himself with a sect or party suited to his spirit and designs, there is no believing his word or oath. If

you read any man partially bitter against others as
differing from him in opinion, or as cross to his greatness, interest or designs, take heed how you believe
any more than the historical evidence, distinct from
his word, compelleth you to believe. The prodigious
lies which have been published in this age in matters
of fact, with unblushing confidence, even where thousands or multitudes of eye and ear-witnesses knew all
to be false, doth call men to take heed what history
they believe, especially where power and violence affordeth that privilege to the reporter, that no man
dare answer him or detect his fraud, or if they do
their writings are all suppressed. As long as men
have liberty to examine and contradict one another,
one may partly conjecture, by comparing their words,
on which side the truth is likely to lie. But when
great men write history, or flatteries by their appoint-
ment, which no man dare contradict, believe it but as
you are constrained. Yet in these cases I can freely
believe history: 1. If the person shew that he is acquainted with what he saith. 2. And if he shew you
the evidences of honesty and conscience, and the fear
of God, which may be much perceived in the spirit
of a writing. 3. And if he appear to be impartial and
charitable, and a lover of goodness and of mankind;
and not possessed with malignity or personal illwill
and malice, nor carried away by faction or personal
interest. Conscionable men dare not lie; but faction
and interest abate men's tenderness of conscience.
And a charitable, impartial heathen may speak truth
in a love to truth and hatred of a lie : but ambitious
malice and false religion will not stick to serve themselves on any thing. It is easy to trace the footsteps
of veracity in the intelligence, impartiality and inge-
nuity of a Thuanus, a Guicciardine, a Paulus Venet,

though Papists, and of Socrates and Sozomen, though
accused by the factious of favouring the Novatians;
and many Protestants in a Melancthon, a Bucholtzer,
and many more; and among physicians in such as
Crato, Platerus, &c. But it is easy to see the footsteps of partiality, and faction, and design, in a Ge-
nebrard, a Baronius, and a multitude of their com-
panions, and to see reason of suspicion in many more.
Therefore I confess I give but halting credit to most
histories that are written, not only against the Albi-
genses and Waldenses, but against most of the ancient heretics, who have left us none of their own
writings in which they speak for themselves, and I
heartily lament that the historical writings of the
ancient schismatics and heretics (as they were called)
perished, and that partiality suffered them not to sur-
vive, that we might have had more light in the church-
affairs of those times, and been better able to judge
between the Fathers and them. And as I am prone
to think that few of them were so bad as their adversaries made them; so I am apt to think that such as
the Novatians, and Luciferians, and Indians, &c.
whom their adversaries condemn, were very good
men, and more godly than most Catholics, however
mistaken in some one point. Sure I am that as the
lies of the Papists, of Luther, Zuinglius, Calvin and
Beza, are visibly malicious and impudent, by the
common plenary contradicting evidence; and yet
the multitude of their seduced ones believe them all
in despite of truth and charity: so in this age there
have been such things written against parties and
persons whom the writers design to make odious,
so notoriously false as you would think that the sense
of their honour at least should have made it impossi-
ble for such men to write. My own eyes have read

such words and actions asserted with most vehement
iterated, unblushing confidence, which abundance of
ear-witnesses, even of their own parties must needs
know to have been altogether false : and therefore
having myself now written this history of myself,
notwithstanding my protestation that I have not in
any thing wilfully gone against the truth, I expect no
more credit from the reader, than the self-evidencing
light of the matter, with concurrent rational advantages, from persons, and things, and other witnesses,
shall constrain him to; if he be a person that is un-
acquainted with the author himself, and the other
evidences of his veracity and credibility. And, I have
purposely omitted almost all the descriptions of any
persons that ever opposed me, or that ever I or my
brethren suffered by, because I know that the appearance of interest and partiality might give a fair excuse to the reader's incredulity : (although indeed the
true description of persons is much of the very life of
history, and especially of the history of the age which
I have lived in ; yet to avoid the suspicion of partiality I have left it out). Except only when I speak of
the Cromwellians and Sectaries, where I am the more
free, because none suspecteth my interest to have engaged me against them ; but (with the rest of my
brethren) I have opposed them in the obedience of
my conscience, when by pleasing them I could have
had almost any thing that they could have given me,
and when beforehand I expected that the present
governors should silence me, and deprive me of maintenance, house and home, as they have done by me
and many hundreds more. Therefore I supposed
that my descriptions and censures of those persons
which would have enriched and honoured me, and of
their actions against that party which hath silenced.

impoverished and accused me, and which beforehand
I expected should do so, are beyond the suspicion of
envy, self-interest or partiality : if not, I there also
am content that the reader exercise his liberty, and
believe no worse even of these men, than the evidence
of fact constraineth him.

Thus much of the alterations of my soul, since my
younger years, I thought best to give the reader, instead of those experiences and actual motions and affections, which I suppose him rather to have expected
an account of. And having transcribed thus much
of a life which God hath read, and conscience hath
read, and must farther read, I humbly lament it, and
beg pardon of it, as sinful, and too unequal and unprofitable : and I warn the reader to amend that in
his own, which he findeth to have been amiss in mine ;
confessing also that much hath been amiss which I
have not here particularly mentioned, and that I have
not lived according to the abundant mercies of the
Lord. But what I have recorded, hath been especially to perform my vows, and declare his praise to
all generations, who hath filled up my days with
his invaluable favours, and bound me to bless his
name for ever : and also to prevent the defective performance of this task by some overvaluing brethren
who I know intended it, and were unfitter to do it
than myself. And for such reasons as Junius, Scultetus, Thuanus, and many others have done the like
before me. The principal of which are these three :
1. As travellers and seamen use to do after great ad-
ventures and deliverances, I hereby satisfy my conscience, in praising the blessed author of all those un-
deserved mercies which have filled up my life. 2.
Foreseeing by the attempts of Bishop Morley, what
Prelatists and Papists are like to say of me, when they

have none to contradict them, and how possible it is that those that never knew me may believe them, though they have lost their hopes with all the rest, I take it to be my duty to be so faithful to that stock of reputation which God hath intrusted me with, as to defend it at the rate of opening the truth. Such as have made the world believe that Luther consulted with the devil, that Calvin was a stigmatized Sodomite, that Beza turned Papist, &c. to blast their labours, I know are very likely to say any thing by me, which their interest or malice tell them will any way advantage their cause, to make my writings unprofitable when I am dead. 3. That young Christians may be warned by the mistakes and failings of my unriper times, to learn in patience, and live in watchfulness, and not to be fierce and proudly confident in their first conceptions ; and to reverence ripe experienced age, and to take heed of taking such for their chief guides as have nothing but immature and inexperienced judgments, with fervent affections, and free and confident expressions ; but to learn of them that have with holiness, study, time and trial, looked about them as well on one side as the other, and attained to clearness and impartiality in their judgments.

1. But having mentioned the changes which I think were for the better, I must add, that as I confessed many of my sins before, so since I have been guilty of many, which because materially they seemed small, have had the less resistance, and yet on the review do trouble more than if they had been greater, done in ignorance : it can be no small sin formally which is committed against knowledge, and conscience, and deliberation, whatever excuse it have. To have sinned while I preached and wrote against

I

sin, and had such abundant and great obligations from
God, and made so many promises against it, doth lay
me very low : not so much in fear of hell, as in great
displeasure against myself, and such self-abhorrence
as would cause revenge upon myself were it not forbidden. When God forgiveth me I cannot forgive myself, especially for any rash words or deeds, by which
I have seemed injurious, and less tender and kind
than I should have been to my near and dear relations,
whose love abundantly obliged me; when such are
dead, though we never differed in point of interest or
any great matter, every sour, or cross provoking
word which I gave them, maketh me almost irrecon-
cileable to myself : and tells me how repentance
brought some of old to pray to the dead whom they had
wronged, to forgive them, in the hurry of their passion.

2. And though I before told the change of my
judgment against provoking writings, I have had
more will than skill since to avoid such. I must
mention it by way of penitent confession, that I am
too much inclined to such words in controversial
writings which are too keen, and apt to provoke the
person whom I write against. Sometimes I suspect
that age soureth my spirits, and sometimes I am apt
to think that it is long thinking and speaking of such
things that maketh me weary, and less patient with
others that understand them not : and sometimes I
am ready to think that it is out of a hatred of the
flattering humour which now prevaileth so in the
world, that few persons are able to bear the truth :
and I am sure that I cannot only bear myself such
language as I use to others, but that I expect it. I
think all these are partly causes ; but I am sure the
principal cause is a long custom of studying how to
speak and write in the keenest manner to the com-

mon, ignorant and ungodly people (without which
keenness to them, no sermon nor book does much
good); which hath so habituated me to it, that I am
still falling into the same with others; forgetting
that many ministers and professors of strictness do
desire the greatest sharpness to the vulgar, and to
their adversaries, and the greatest lenity, and smooth-
ness, and comfort, if not honour to themselves. And
I have a strong natural inclination to speak of every
subject just as it is, and to call a spade a spade,
' et verba rebus aptare;' so as that the thing spoken
of may be most fully known by the words, which
methinks is part of our speaking truly. But I unfeignedly confess that it is faulty, because imprudent; (for that is not a good means which doth harm,
because it is not fitted to the end;) and because
whilst the readers think me angry, (though I feel no
passion at such times in myself) it is scandalous and
a hindrance to the usefulness of what I write: and
especially because (though I feel no anger, yet which
is worse) I know that there is some want of honour
and love or tenderness to others; or else I should not
be apt to use such words as open their weakness and
offend them: and therefore I repent of it, and wish
all over-sharp passages were expunged from my
writings, and desire forgiveness of God and man.
And yet I must say, that I am oft afraid of the contrary extreme, lest when I speak against great and
dangerous errors and sins, (though of persons otherwise honest) I should encourage men to them, by
speaking too easily of them (as Eli did to his sons),
and lest I should so favour the person as may befriend
the sin, and wrong the church. And I must say, as
the New England Synodists in their defence against
Mr. Davenport, " We heartily desire that as much as

may be, all expressions and reflections may be forborn that tend to break the bond of love. Indeed such is our infirmity, that the naked discovery of the fallacy or invalidity of another's allegations or arguings is apt to provoke. This in disputes is unavoidable."

And therefore I am less for a disputing way than ever; believing that it tempteth men to bend their wits, to defend their errors and oppose the truth, and hindereth usually their information : and the servant of the Lord must not strive, but be gentle to all men, &c. Therefore I am most in judgment for a learning or a teaching way of converse. In all companies I will be glad either to hear those speak that can teach me, or to be heard of those that have need to learn.

. And that which I named before on the by, is grown one of my great diseases. I have lost much of that zeal which I had, to propagate any truths to others, save the mere fundamentals. When I perceive people or ministers (which is too common) to think they know what indeed they do not, and to dispute those things which they never thoroughly studied, or expect I should debate the case with them, as if an hour's talk would serve instead of an acute understanding and seven years' study, I have no zeal to make them of my opinion, but an impatience of continuing discourse with them on such subjects, and am apt to be silent or to turn to something else : which (though there be some reason for it) I feel cometh from a want of zeal for the truth, and from an impatient temper of mind. I am ready to think that people should quickly understand all in a few words ; and if they cannot, lazily to despair of them, and leave them to themselves. And I the more know that it is sinful in me, because it is partly so in other things ; even about the faults of my servants or other inferiora, if three or four times warning do no good on them, I am much tempted to despair of them, and turn them away, and leave them to themselves.

I mention all these distempers, that my faults may be a warning to others to take heed, as they call on myself for repentance and watchfulness. O Lord, for the merits, and sacrifice, and intercession of Christ, be merciful to me a sinner, and forgive my known and unknown sins.

MR. BAXTER'S CHARACTER:

As given in a Funeral Sermon preached by Mr. Matthew Sylvester.

"MR. RICHARD BAXTER was a person deservedly of great fame and character in his day. He seemed to be a transcript of what is left upon record concerning *St. Paul, Sylvanus*, and *Timothy*, in 1 Thess. ii. 1—12. It is evident he was a man of God, a Gospel-prophet. He was furnished for, fervent in, painful about, and faithful to, his ministerial trust and work; and extraordinary in the evident acceptance and successes of his ministerial labours. A man of clear, deep, fixed thoughts; a man of copious and well digested reading; a man of ready, free, and very proper elocution; and aptly expressive of his own thoughts and sentiments. He was most intent upon the weightiest and most useful parts of learning; yet a great lover of all kinds and degrees thereof. He could, in preaching, writing, conference, accommodate himself to all capacities; and answer his obligations to the wise and unwise. He had a moving *rôles* and useful acrimony in his words; neither did his expressions want their emphatical accent, as the matter did require. And when he spake of weighty soul-concerns, you might find his very spirit drenched therein. He was pleasingly conversible, save in his studying hours, wherein he could not bear with trivial disturbances. He was sparingly facetious; but never light or frothy. His heart was warm, plain, fixed: his life was blameless, exemplary, uniform. He was unmoveable, where apprehensive of his duty; yet affable and condescending, where likelihood of doing good was in his prospect. His personal abstinence, severities and labours were exceeding great: he kept his body under, and always feared pampering his flesh too much. He diligently and with great pleasure minded his master's work within doors and without, while he was able. His charity was very great: greatly proportionable to his abilities; his purse was ever open to the poor; and, where the case required it, he never thought great sums too much: he rather gave *cumulatim* than *denariatim*; and suited what he gave, to the necessities and characters of those he gave to: nor was his charity confined to parties or opinions. He was a man of manifold and pressing exercises; and of answerable patience and submission under the hand of God; and though he was seldom without pain or sickness (but mostly pain), yet never did he murmur; but used to say, ' It is but flesh.' And when I have asked him how he did, his usual answer was, either ' Almost well,' or, ' Better than I deserve to be; but not so well as I hope to be.' Once, I remember, when I was with him in the country at his request, he (being in the extremity of pain, and that so exquisite as to appear in the sudden and great changes of his countenance) raised himself from his couch whereon he had laid himself, and thus expressed himself, ' Whatever the world thinks of me, I can truly say, that I have served God with uprightness of heart, and that I never

spake any thing that I took not to be truth, and at
that time to be my duty.' He was no ways clandes-
tinely rigid or censorious as to others. When he told
men to their faces of their faults he would hear what
they had to say, and then reprove them with as great
pungency as he thought their fault deserved ; but yet
behind men's backs he was always ready to believe
the best; and whatever he could think on that might
extenuate their crime, if there was any likelihood of
truth therein, he would be sure to mention that : so
great a friend was he to every man's useful reputation. As to himself, even to the last, I never could
perceive his peace and heavenly hopes assaulted or
disturbed. I have often heard him greatly lament
himself, in that he felt no greater liveliness in what
appeared so great and clear to him, and so very much
desired by him. As to the influence thereof upon
his spirit, in order to the sensible refreshments of it,
he clearly saw what ground he had to rejoice in God ;
he doubted not of his right to heaven : he told me,
he knew it should be well with him when he was
gone. He wondered to hear others speak of their so
sensible, passionately strong desires to die; and of
their transports of spirit when sensible of their approaching death : when as he himself thought he
knew as much as they ; and had as rational satisfaction as they could have that his soul was safe : and
yet could never feel their sensible consolations. And
when I asked him, whether much of this was not
to be resolved into bodily constitution ; he did indeed tell me, that he thought *it might be so*. But
I have often thought, that God wisely made him
herein (as in many other things) conformable to his
great Master Jesus Christ ; whose joys we find commonly the fruit of deep and close thought. Christ

argued himself into his own comforts. Which thing
is evident from Scriptures not a few; take for a taste,
Psal. xvi. 8—11. Heb. xii. 2. The testimony of
his conscience was ever his rejoicing; like that in
2 Cor. i. 12. He ever kept that tender; and gave
such diligence to run his race, fulfil his ministry, and
so make his calling and election firm and clear, as
that I cannot but conclude, an entrance was minis-
tered abundantly to his departed spirit into the everlasting kingdom of his God and Saviour, and that it
will be more abundant to his raised person when
the Lord appears.

On Tuesday morning about four o'clock, December
8, 1691, he expired; though he expected and desired
his dissolution to have been on the Lord's-day before,
which with joy, to me, he called a *high day*, because
of his desired change expected then by him. He had
frequently before his death owned to me his conti-
nuance in the same sentiments that he had discovered
to the world before in his polemical discourses, especially about justification, and the covenants of
works and grace, &c. And being asked at my request, whether he had changed his former thoughts
about those things; his answer was, 'That he had
told the world sufficiently his judgment concerning
them by words and writing, and thither he referred
men.' And then lifting up his eyes to heaven, he uttered these words; 'Lord, pity, pity, pity the ignorance of this poor city.' About five o'clock the pre-
ceding evening, Death sent his harbinger to summon
him away. A great trembling and coldness seized
him, and extorted strong cries to Heaven for pity and
redress; after which he lay in an observant, patient
expectation of his change. Being asked by his at-
tendant whether he knew her or not, requesting some

signification of it if he did, he softly cried, *death, death*. The last words that he spake to me (being informed that I was come to see him) were these, ' O I thank him, I thank him :' and turning his eyes to me, he said, ' The Lord teach you to die.'

Thus lived and died this excellent and holy man. In his person he was tall and slender, and stooped much; his countenance composed and grave, somewhat inclining to smile. He had a piercing eye, a very articulate speech, and his deportment rather plain than complimental. He had a great command over his thoughts. He had that happy faculty, so as to answer the character that was given of him by a learned man dissenting from him, after discourse with him; which was, that *He could say what he would, and he could prove what he said.*'

Dr. Bates also in a Funeral Sermon for Mr. Baxter, speaks of him as follows :

" Not long after his last sermon, he felt the approaches of death, and was confined to his sick bed. Death reveals the secrets of the heart, then words are spoken with most feeling and least affectation. This excellent saint was the same in his life and death : his last hours were spent in preparing others and himself to appear before God. He said to his friends that visited him, ' You come hither to learn to die ; I am not the only person that must go this way : I can assure you that your whole life, be it never so long, is little enough to prepare for death. Have a care of this vain, deceitful world, and the lusts of the flesh : be sure you choose God for your portion, heaven for your hope, God's glory for your end, his word for your rule, and then you need never fear but we shall meet with comfort.'

Many times he prayed, " God be merciful to me a

sinner," and blessed God that that was left upon record in the Gospel as an effectual prayer. He said, 'God may justly condemn me for the best duty I ever did: and all my hopes are from the free mercy of God in Christ,' which he often prayed for.

After a slumber, he waked and said, 'I shall rest from my labour.' A minister then present said, And your works follow you: to whom he replied, 'No works, I will leave out works, if God will grant me the other.' When a friend was comforting him with the remembrance of the good many had received by his preaching and writings, he said, 'I was but a pen in God's hand, and what praise is due to a pen?'

His resigned submission to the will of God in his sharp sickness, was eminent. When extremity of pain constrained him earnestly to pray to God for his release by death, he would check himself: 'It is not fit for me to prescribe;' and said, 'When thou wilt, what thou wilt, how thou wilt.'

Being in great anguish, he said, 'O how unsearchable are his ways, and his paths past finding out; the reaches of his providence we cannot fathom!' and to his friends, 'Do not think the worse of religion for what you see me suffer.'

Being often asked by his friends, how it was with his inward man, he replied, 'I bless God I have a well-grounded assurance of my eternal happiness, and great peace and comfort within;' but it was his trouble he could not triumphantly express it, by reason of his extreme pains. He said, 'Flesh must perish, and we must feel the perishing of it: and that though his judgment submitted, yet sense would still make him groan.

Being asked by a person of quality, whether he had not great joy from his believing apprehensions of the invisible state, he replied : 'What else think you Christianity serves for ?' He said, 'The consideration of the Deity in his glory and greatness was too high for our thoughts : but the consideration of the Son of God in our nature, and of the saints in heaven, whom he knew and loved, did much sweeten and familiarize heaven to him.' The description of heaven in Heb. xii. 22, was most comfortable to him : That he was going " to the innumerable company of angels, and to the general assembly and church of the firstborn, whose names are written in heaven ; and to God the judge of all, and to the spirits of just men made perfect ; and to Jesus the Mediator of the New Covenant, and to the blood of sprinkling that speaketh better things than the blood of Abel." ' That Scripture,' he said, ' deserved a thousand thousand thoughts.' He said, ' O how comfortable is that promise, " Eye hath not seen, nor ear heard, neither hath it entered into the heart of man to conceive the things God hath laid up for those who love him." '

At another time he said, 'That he found great comfort and sweetness in repeating the words of the Lord's Prayer, and was sorry that some good people were prejudiced against the use of it ; for there were all necessary petitions for soul and body contained in it.'

At other times he gave excellent counsel to young ministers that visited him, and earnestly prayed to God to bless their labours, and make them very successful in converting many souls to Christ.

He did often pray that God would be merciful to this miserable, distracted world : and that he would preserve his church and interest in it.

He advised his friends to beware of self-conceitedness, as a sin that was likely to ruin this nation ;

and said, 'I have written a book against it, which I am afraid has done little good.'

I went to him with a very worthy friend, *Mr. Mather* of New England, the day before he died, and speaking some comforting words to him, he replied, 'I have pain, there is no arguing against sense, but I have peace; I have peace.' I told him, 'You are now approaching to your long-desired home;' he answered, 'I believe, I believe.' He said to *Mr. Mather,* 'I bless God that you have accomplished your business: the Lord prolong your life.'

He expressed a great willingness to die; and during his sickness, when the question was asked, how he did, his reply was, 'Almost well.' His joy was most remarkable, when in his own apprehensions death was nearest: and his spiritual joy at length was consummate in eternal joy.

Thus lived and died that blessed saint. I have, without any artificial fiction of words, given a sincere short account of him. All our tears are below the just grief for such an invaluable loss. It is the comfort of his friends, that he enjoys a blessed reward in heaven, and has left a precious remembrance on the earth.

May I live the short remainder of my life, as entirely to the glory of God, as he lived; and when I shall come to the period of my life, may I die in the same blessed peace wherein he died; may I be with him in the kingdom of light and love for ever!"

FINIS.

Richard Edwards, Printer, Crane-court, Fleet-street, London.

CPSIA information can be obtained at www.ICGtesting.com
Printed in the USA
LVOW020301041212

309909LV00018B/904/P